What your colleagues are saying . . .

"After 30 years in education, I rarely come across books that provide new ideas and provoke strong debate among my colleagues. This is one such book. It is filled with stories and linked knowledge—crucial information, really—that reflects the reality and truth of our relationships in schools. The stories are told with nuance and grace and demand attention, consideration, and conversation in order to increase the odds that schools can truly continue to develop better humans—students and their teachers alike—every day. The authors live this truth. I believe them, and I aspire to work with a fraction of their intensity, knowledge, passion, and skill to serve young adults and grown-up educators."

Sam Bennett
Instructional Coach, Education Consultant, Author of
That Workshop Book

"This is an invaluable resource for teachers and administrators who are serving students who experience chronic stress and trauma. Each chapter provides real-world examples, resources, and strategies that can be implemented immediately in order to mitigate the impact of chronic stress for both teachers and students."

Jennifer Craft
Supervisor, Secondary English Language Arts and Literacy,
Montgomery County Public Schools

"*Teaching, Learning, and Trauma* is for educators who are in the trenches with students who have experienced chronic stress. While educators have always had to deal with a few students who have chronic stress, the number has risen dramatically. This book provides excellent guidance to educators around navigating trauma and stress in their classrooms."

Dominique Cooper
Teacher, Eastern Middle School

"Authors Brooke O'Drobinak and Beth Kelley have a genuine, warm approach to topics educators have wrestled with over the years. This book uses stories that one can relate to and that are relevant to all educators, especially at the secondary level where teens are experiencing trauma and schools are not equipped to handle it."

Sari Glazebrook
LCSW, CADC, EMDR Trained, North Suburban
Special Education District

"This book is highly relevant to the changing landscape of teaching and learning. Teaching with trauma-informed practices is extremely important and necessary for today's learners. The authors offer practical strategies to help teachers create a safe environment for all students . . . and themselves."

Brenda Green
Staff Development Teacher, Cabin John Middle School

"Successful schools are not transactional. Rather, they operate as healthy communities where teachers and students understand one another as people and, from that foundation, build meaningful working relationships. In their new book, *Teaching, Learning, and Trauma*, O'Drobinak and Kelley offer teachers and administrators the practical tools necessary to build these types of school communities. Thoughtfully grounded in the realities of the classroom, the book explores real-world scenarios with which each of us is familiar and provides an account of how to transform those challenging classroom experiences into opportunities for lasting professional growth."

Michael J. O'Hagan
President, Arrupe Jesuit High School

"*Teaching, Learning, and Trauma* offers a compelling message of hope for educators across all disciplines. It moves from an idea to implementation and is easy to read for busy educators. It offers practical solutions for facilitating the process of handling chronic stress in schools and is the one tool that will enhance the culture and performance of one's school."

Debra Paradowski
Associate Principal, Arrowhead Union High School

"*Teaching, Learning, and Trauma* is well written, with strong examples and clear expertise of the subject matter from the authors. This book aims to sincerely help educators."

Steve Reifman
NBC Elementary School Teacher & Author,
Santa Monica-Malibu USD

"Emotional trauma can influence all parts of the school experience for both students and adults. This book is a great resource and a reminder of the importance of building relationships."

Lena Marie Rockwood
Assistant Principal, Revere High School

"I recommend *Teaching, Learning, and Trauma* for professional development for schools or systems that have not provided training on this topic or in the area of equity."

Farhana N. Shah
Teacher and Department Chair for ESOL and World Languages,
Montgomery County Public Schools

"This book goes beyond giving tips on classroom management. The authors do a great job of focusing not just on student stress, but also on teacher stress and how to mitigate it. They give the educator an opportunity to step into a student's shoes while bringing in cultural awareness that extends across all races and socioeconomic classes."

Kendra Simmons
Educational Consultant, Center for the Advancement of
Transformative Education (CATE)

"Oh boy, do I need this book! If you work with teens, you know they can be quirky. Add chronic stress and trauma to the mix, and one can feel at a loss as to how to keep the teaching and learning going. If this is a trend you are noticing, this book will not only explain why teens act the way they do, but also provide instructional strategies that honor and harness their behaviors—and your own—to keep engagement high. The authors help readers understand the science behind teen behaviors, provide useful strategies to re-engage students, and give you hope that you can continue to do the job you love of teaching teens! *Teaching, Learning, and Trauma* is a must-have for any educator working with adolescents—a just-right book for our complicated times."

Cris Tovani
Teacher, Author of *I Read It but I Don't Get It*

Teaching, Learning, and Trauma

Grades 6–12

Teaching, Learning, and Trauma

Responsive Practices for Holding Steady in Turbulent Times

Grades 6–12

Brooke O'Drobinak and Beth Kelley

Foreword by Diane Sweeney

FOR INFORMATION:

Corwin

A SAGE Company

2455 Teller Road

Thousand Oaks, California 91320

(800) 233-9936

www.corwin.com

SAGE Publications Ltd.

1 Oliver's Yard

55 City Road

London, EC1Y 1SP

United Kingdom

SAGE Publications India Pvt. Ltd.

B 1/I 1 Mohan Cooperative Industrial Area

Mathura Road, New Delhi 110 044

India

SAGE Publications Asia-Pacific Pte. Ltd.

18 Cross Street #10-10/11/12

China Square Central

Singapore 048423

Publisher: Jessica Allan

Senior Content Development
   Editor: Lucas Schleicher

Associate Content Development
   Editor: Mia Rodriguez

Production Editor: Tori Mirsadjadi

Copy Editor: Will DeRooy

Typesetter: Hurix Digital

Proofreader: Alison Syring

Indexer: Integra

Cover Designer: Gail Buschman

Marketing Manager: Olivia Bartlett

Library of Congress Cataloging-in-Publication Data

Names: O'Drobinak, Brooke, author. | Kelley, Beth (Psychotherapist) author.

Title: Teaching, learning, and trauma : responsive practices for holding steady in turbulent times, grades 6-12 / Beth Kelley and Brooke O'Drobinak ; Foreword by Diane Sweeney.

Description: Thousand Oaks, California : Corwin Press, [2021] | Includes bibliographical references.

Identifiers: LCCN 2020017429 | ISBN 9781544362892 (paperback) | ISBN 9781544364056 (epub) | ISBN 9781544364087 (epub) | ISBN 9781544364070 (ebook)

Subjects: LCSH: Students with social disabilities—Education (Middle school) | Students with social disabilities—Education (Secondary) | Psychic trauma in adolescence. | Youth—Mental health services.

Classification: LCC LC4069.3 .O37 2020 | DDC 371.826/94Ædc23

LC record available at https://lccn.loc.gov/2020017429

This book is printed on acid-free paper.

20 21 22 23 24 10 9 8 7 6 5 4 3 2 1

Contents

Foreword

According to a recent study by the Pew Research Center, anxiety and depression rank as the biggest problem teens see among their peers, with 70% seeing them as a major concern. According to the study, "Concern about mental health cuts across gender, racial and socio-economic lines, with roughly equal shares of teens across demographic groups saying it is a significant issue in their community" (Pew Research Center Survey of U.S. Teens Ages 13–17, 2018). In my work with leaders and instructional coaches across the secondary landscape, I am struck by the urgency around this issue. If we hope to get this right, it means we must equip teachers to support their students as both people and learners. We must also consider how school policies can promote and cultivate this important work.

Teaching, Learning, and Trauma: Responsive Practices for Holding Steady in Turbulent Times by Brooke O'Drobinak and Beth Kelley is a book that tackles these challenges from two vantage points. Brooke O'Drobinak has been a middle- and high school educator for more than 20 years. More recently, she has served as a leader in curriculum and instruction in a high school in Denver, Colorado. In this role, she focused on supporting teachers, developing curriculum, and designing a healthy school culture. Beth Kelley is a psychotherapist who was a school-based counselor for more than 15 years, and she brings both a therapeutic perspective and a background in how trauma, biology, and developmental factors influence the lives of adolescents. Together, they have crafted a book that addresses how we can better design schools for the adolescents we serve.

As a mother of two teens, I wish my children could have the opportunity to be in schools like the ones that Brooke and Beth describe in this book. If this were the case, I would be confident that the teachers in their lives understand them as complex individuals who carry a heavy burden of what it's like to be a teen in today's turbulent times. Brené Brown reminds us that our connection with students is about building *belonging* first. When we take this approach, we are more able to move toward the acquisition of learning for all students. To make this happen, the authors provide instructional strategies and practices that are built on a foundation of *empathy* and *rigor*. By taking this approach, they frame how we can design schools to not only meet the needs of our students, but also help them thrive as humans. We aren't talking about scraping together grant funding to offer meditation and yoga classes during advisory class and then changing nothing else. It's bigger than that.

The authors paint a picture through stories and anecdotes that illustrate the complexity of this work. They also provide strategies and solutions that are framed through both the adult and the student experience. This serves as a reminder that while it's essential to take care of our students, we must also take care of ourselves. After all, we carry a heavy a burden as well.

The bottom line is whatever we do in today's schools must propel student learning forward. Having spent decades as a practitioner, author, and coach, I have come to understand the importance of putting student learning front and center. This led me to develop a model for instructional coaching known as Student-Centered Coaching. We must constantly ask ourselves, "Are the students at the center of this conversation?" This book lives up to that promise, because it's about improving the academic and inner lives of students. It's a must-read for any educator who works with adolescents. To be clear, our students need us to read this book.

Diane Sweeney

Author of *The Essential Guide for Student-Centered Coaching* (2020), *Leading Student-Centered Coaching* (2018), and *Student-Centered Coaching: The Moves* (2017)

Preface

Our Journey and Our Hopes for This Book

This book is the culmination of 12 years of partnership, exploration, trial and error, learning, and grace. Our work was made possible by incredible administrators and committed, passionate colleagues, who valued an integrated approach and encouraged us to collaborate, innovate, and grow. Along the way, we have witnessed the transformative power of an integrated model and its benefits for students, families, and educators. We have seen it. We know it is possible. We are truly grateful for the people whom we have loved, respected, and learned so much from during our time together.

We are the first to express the difficulty that belies work of this scope. Simultaneously, we enthusiastically express the possibility that results from approaching education from this standpoint. To be holistic in one's perspective requires great courage and perseverance. We know it can happen for you—and for your students.

Our hope for this book is that it serves educators like you as you go about serving students. Our admiration for you is limitless. The world is made a better place because of your contribution. Thank you.

Acknowledgments

This book is the product of unrelenting encouragement from many people who have ceaselessly inspired, cajoled, and nudged us along the way. First, we offer gratitude to the amazing team of friends, colleagues, and students at Arrupe Jesuit High School, whom we had the pleasure of learning and growing with for so many years. Our hearts are always with you.

This book would not have been possible without the mentorship and support of Diane Sweeney, who said to us, "You have to write a book," and then stuck with us until the end. Thanks to Sam and the Radishes for your no-holds-barred feedback and fierce love.

Special thanks to Bill Grimmer for converting our chicken-scratch into clean diagrams for the digital age.

Last, thanks to Jessica, Mia, Lucas, Will, and the rest of the Corwin team for believing in us and guiding us through this labor of love.

From Brooke

This project reflects the love and commitment of people for whom I am deeply grateful. Thank you, Jon, for your partnership, for holding down the fort, and for being my wingman. Thank you, Luke and Liam, for continually inspiring me to be a better person and for motivating me to improve the world for kids like you. I am indebted to my parents, friends, colleagues, students, and community, who make me who I am. Finally, Beth, thank you for being my writing buddy. You continue to inspire me and encourage me.

From Beth

Writing a book is a humbling task. Among the many lessons learned, I am left with the greatest gift of all: gratitude. First, for my husband, whose encouragement and support has been unwavering. For my friends and my family, who have been my role models, mentors, and cheerleaders. For Brooke, who has inspired me with her brilliant mind and compassionate heart. And for the students I have had the honor to work with—I am forever changed by your courage, resilience, humor, and hope. You give me faith in the future of our world.

Publisher's Acknowledgments

Corwin gratefully acknowledges the contributions of the following reviewers:

Sari Glazebrook
LCSW, CADC, EMDR Trained
NSSED (North Suburban Special Education District)
Highland Park, IL

Brenda Green
Staff Development Teacher
Cabin John Middle School
Potomac, MD

Susan Kessler
Executive Principal
Hunters Lane High School
Nashville, TN

Debra Paradowski
Associate Principal
Arrowhead Union High School
Hartland, WI

Lena Marie Rockwood
Assistant Principal
Revere High School
Revere, MA

Farhana N. Shah
Teacher and Department Chair for ESOL and World Languages
Montgomery County Public Schools
Rockville, MD

About the Authors

Brooke O'Drobinak, MA, has been in secondary education for more than 25 years. Most recently, she has served in school administration for the past 13 years at a high-functioning, inner-city Denver high school. Her work is founded on the belief that students and relationships are at the heart of school communities. She also deeply values the critical roles that professional learning and leadership play in supporting all student learning. She currently provides consulting services for Diane Sweeney Consulting, Corwin, and the Public Education & Business Coalition. When she isn't working with schools and districts, she enjoys being outdoors in Colorado with her husband and two sons.

Beth Kelley, MA, LPC, is a psychotherapist who worked as a school-based therapist for nearly 20 years. Additionally, she has worked in community mental health, in private practice, and as a clinical supervisor. Currently, Beth is a leadership coach and an educational consultant for schools interested in developing a more holistic school model. Beth is deeply committed to supporting mental wellness in school communities and businesses. When she isn't working, she is hanging out with people she loves, laughing, creating, and chillin'.

Introduction

This book is about creating schools that neutralize chronic stress on teachers and students so that learning and achievement become possible. A fundamental belief of a school model that integrates effective practices in teaching, learning, and mental health is that strong and healthy relationships between students and adults in a school result in safe, joyful, and effective learning environments. The integrated student learning model blends effective practices in both teaching and learning with mental health practices, focusing on the impact of trauma in education. The combination of the two critical areas fosters an environment where teachers and students experience results in academic and interpersonal arenas—contributing to a healthy school culture.

This book is our contribution to the conversation about the impact of chronic stress and trauma in secondary education. It is meant not to be prescriptive, but as a comprehensive guide to designing healthier schools. *Teaching, Learning, and Trauma* is timely, especially given the turbulent nature of modern, everyday life.

The Intersection of Teaching, Learning, and Mental Health

This book blends best practices of teaching and learning with trauma-informed perspectives. This integrated approach seeks to mitigate disruptions—such as performance demands, competition, illness, family stress, financial distress, social pressure, natural disasters, political climate, chronic stress, and even the various combined and pervasive disruptions caused by a pandemic—that destabilize a healthy school environment.

We will examine this model through student, teacher, and leadership viewpoints, fortifying the connections that are essential for success from each vantage point. We will provide tools to promote practices that assist practitioners in creating a blended model that can easily adapt to any school design.

The Integrated Approach: Using the Five Lenses

Conceptually, this integrated model can be constructed using five lenses through which teaching, learning, and mental health practices come together: *knowing, planning, being, delivering,* and *partnering.* Together, they provide a comprehensive approach to impact student learning, which will be thoroughly outlined in Chapter 7, "Blending It All Together," where each lens is brought into focus through a teacher-student

Figure 0.1   The Integrated Model

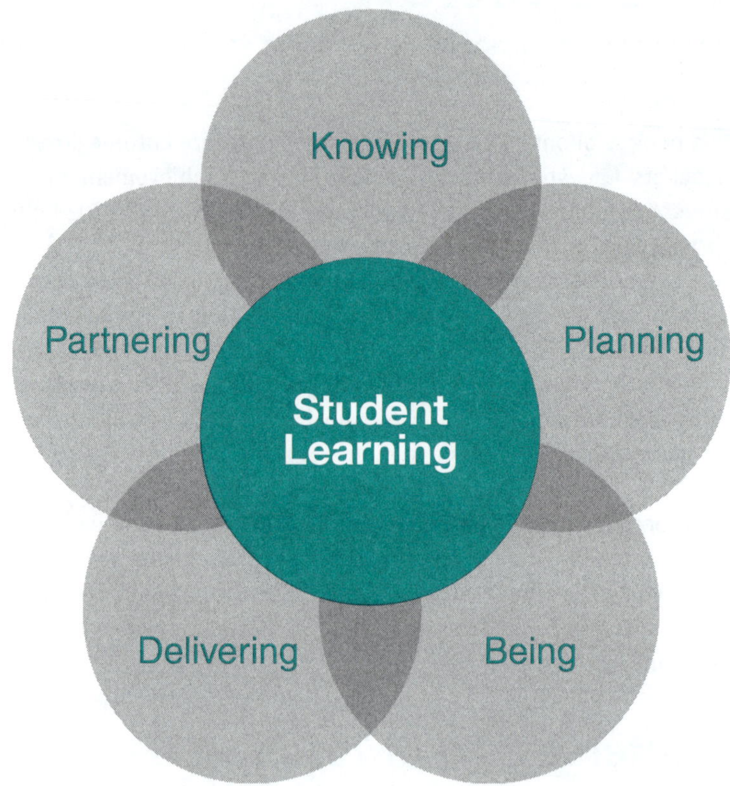

Source: Figure layout by Bill Grimmer.

interaction. An important premise of the integrated model is that all aspects of a school work together to support the whole student.

Intended Audience and Outcome

This book is intended to support those individuals who are seeking to teach adolescents and foster mental wellness in order to create integrated schools to combat chronic stress and trauma. This includes teachers, counselors, instructional coaches, principals, and district leadership. We are all in this together. We like to say, "No one has it all figured out." Our hope is to provide our combined experience and propose ideas to help educators understand students with trauma more deeply, so that they can be effective and cultivate joy in their work.

Organizational Features of This Book

We have identified chapter topics that we and our colleagues have wrestled with over the years. Each chapter provides several glimpses into the everyday world of secondary education through stories of students and adults. You will find that each chapter offers insight into the student and adult experience that result from these interactions. Next, regarding each chapter topic, we aim to answer: "Why Is It Important?" Following, we outline the psychosocial "Foundations for Effective Practice" in order to build a rationale for the practices outlined in "What Works in the Classroom." Subsequently, we offer school leaders considerations for "Taking It School-Wide" in order to build capacity and sustainability. Next, as a means for you to ponder your experience with these ideas, and begin to implement them, we provide Reflections and a "Toolkit for Tomorrow." Finally, we offer some encouraging words to fellow practitioners through the last section, entitled "In the End, Be Loving."

Why This Book, and Why Now?

There are real struggles facing kids, parents, and teachers that seep into and sometimes flood our schools. Chronic stress and trauma exist in all strata of our society, and their impact is overwhelming. The good news is that systems are starting to shift. There is a willingness in school communities to create awareness and implement trauma-informed practices to help mitigate the effects of these stressors.

As we take a look at the ever-increasing contributors to chronic stress and trauma that make things so complicated for teachers and students today, we see the real-world impact on students' physical, emotional, and spiritual well-being: Students can't seem to control their bodies, moods, and emotions. They show up unable to focus, anxious, and depressed. They share stories of abuse and neglect. Ultimately, these factors impact student learning. We are not saying that chronic stress is the root of all the issues that teachers face; however, if you are willing to look at the data with an open mind, we think you'll begin to shift the lens through which you see your students, and then change will be possible.

Yes, things are hard—yet there is hope, and real changes are happening. In order to be a part of the change you wish to see, you have to take an honest look at what is happening for students and educators in your school. You can't address what you haven't named—so, although you may find this content hard to read (because it is sad and disheartening), you need to face the reality of it in order to reshape the present and future.

Essential Background Knowledge: ACEs

As you read this book, it will be helpful to understand adverse childhood experiences (ACEs) and the role they play in schools.

The basis of most literature related to chronic stress and trauma in children includes the CDC–Kaiser Permanente (ACEs) Study, one of the largest investigations of the effects of childhood abuse and neglect on later-life health and well-being. The original ACEs Study was conducted at Kaiser Permanente from 1995 to 1997; it included 17,300 participants and shows a correlation between adverse childhood experiences and an increase of social, emotional, and health problems as an adult (CDC, 1997).

Below is a list of the top 10 ACEs (from Sporleder & Forbes, 2016) that correlate to an increase of behavior and health issues later in life.

Top 10 List of Adverse Childhood Experiences

1. **Sexual abuse:** any act of sexual nature that uses the child for sexual gratification of the adult, including rape, molestation, prostitution, pornography, or other forms of sexual exploitation of children

2. **Physical abuse:** generally defined as any non-accidental physical injury to the child, including striking, kicking, burning, or biting the child, or any action that results in a physical impairment or harms the child's health and welfare

3. **Emotional abuse:** emotional or psychological injury to the child as evidenced by a substantial change in behavior, emotional response or anxiety, depression, withdrawal, or aggressive behavior

4. **Physical neglect:** the failure of a parent or caregiver to provide food, clothing, shelter, education, medical care, or supervision such that the child's health, safety, and well-being are threatened with harm

5. **Emotional neglect:** the failure of a parent to provide needed emotional attention, support, recognition, love, and empathetic response such that the child's emotional health and development are threatened with harm

6. **Loss of a parent:** discontinuation of contact with a parent due to death, divorce, or abandonment

7. **Witnessing family violence:** being a witness to violence creates significant emotional and psychological damage due to the high stress experienced by the child

8. **Incarceration of a family member:** the experience of having any family member in jail can create substantial emotional issues, such as grief and loss, stigmatization, anxiety, and depression

9. **Having a mentally ill, depressed, or suicidal family member:** growing up in a family dealing with mental health issues can cause confusion, fear, anxiety, stress, and lack of attention and concern regarding the child's own emotional healthw

10. **Living with a drug-addicted or alcoholic family member:** drug and alcohol addiction of parents can negatively impact a child's sense of safety, predictability, stability, normalcy, connectedness, and attachment

ACEs Score: ______________________

Source: Sporleder and Forbes, *The Trauma-Informed School: A Step-by-Step Implementation Guide for Administrators and School Personnel.* Beyond Consequences Institute, LLC, 2016.

If you want to test yourself, simply give yourself one point for each of the ACEs that you experienced from birth to 18 years of age. Add them up and you have your ACEs score.

In the absence of caring adult intervention, an ACEs score of 6 or greater can have a negative impact on your overall life expectancy and general well-being. Taking an assessment like this, or reading this book for that matter, might prove upsetting to some readers. If taking inventory of your own ACEs upsets you, please seek some support for yourself, or take care of yourself in a way that honors what you need. You deserve it.

The ACEs Study has uncovered how ACEs are strongly related to development of risk factors for disease and reduced well-being throughout the lifespan. A person with a higher number of adverse childhood experiences goes through life in a more vulnerable and less secure way than someone with a lower number. Imagine how this difference plays out for children in a classroom or school environment. We will be referring to these definitions throughout the course of this book to explain and explore the places where trauma, teaching, and learning connect.

The Impact of ACEs on Learning

Chronic stress and ACEs impact learning in a number of ways. You can imagine the biological, emotional, and spiritual impact from trauma on the developing child. Trauma shows up in a classroom in a multitude of ways. Students who have been traumatized most likely get overwhelmed and confused easily, are slower to process information, and have poor problem-solving skills. For a full list of impacts of ACEs on learning, see *The Trauma-Informed School* by Jim Sporleder and Heather Forbes (2016).

You will experience real change when you join the quest to create a school that integrates teaching, learning, and mental health. Combating chronic stress and trauma is not easy. It will take a shift in your perception, your mindset, and your practices. And by focusing on the what, the why, and the how, you will surely be able to connect or reconnect with the joys of teaching. Maintaining healthy relationships and being an effective teacher in today's stressful times requires a reimagining of what is possible for students and for you.

In Their Natural Habitat

Understanding and Teaching Adolescent Learners With Chronic Stress and Trauma

CHAPTER 1

> *"Be yourself; everyone else is already taken."*
> **—Oscar Wilde**

"You don't understand!" Jackie yelled at the counselor, her pupils dilated. The counselor watched as the red splotches at the nape of Jackie's neck slowly crept up toward her cheeks. Her breath was shallow, and the tears rolled down her face onto her shirt. "What is the big deal? This isn't fair! Why am I the one who got in trouble when everyone else did it too?!" Her shoulders shook as she sobbed. The counselor sat still in the chair across from Jackie, while fear and sadness engulfed the small office. The counselor glanced over at Jackie's parents and her teacher. Their eyes were fixed on the counselor, searching for guidance and understanding. The counselor had seen this look many times over the years from adults desperate for help, insight, or even a simple explanation: *Why would she do it? What was she thinking? What had happened to our sweet, compliant, fun-loving child?* And for a short time, which felt like a long time, they all sat silent, no one wanting to make a wrong move.

Understanding Adolescent Learners With Chronic Stress and Trauma: Why Is It Important?

Chronic stress and trauma relentlessly bombard young people as they try to figure out their way in today's world. It's overwhelming. Adverse Childhood Experiences (Centers for Disease Control and Prevention, 2019), poverty, helicopter parents, social media, pressure to succeed, and isolation are just some of the factors contributing to the chronic stress and trauma that is palpable in schools today. Teachers are often expected to attend to students' mental health needs, yet they have little training or support in that area. They are overworked, under-resourced, and spread thin. Yet, something drew you to work with adolescents, in a school: This work is not for the faint of heart or the thin-skinned. In this chapter, we will explore the unique strengths and challenges that come with adolescence and will provide you with strategies and practices that create the possibility of dynamic, successful education in the face of chronic stress and trauma.

Adolescence is a time of great transition and growth. There are tremendous changes happening: biological, relational, emotional, spiritual, moral, and psychological. Add chronic stress and trauma to the "normal" adolescent experience, and surviving adolescence is, in itself, a rite of passage.

Let's begin by looking at the picture of an adolescent with chronic stress and trauma, first from the student's experience of it and then from the teacher's (yours).

Student Experience

Shelly is a high school junior who excels in language arts. She is always tired in the mornings and frequently arrives late to school because she relies on her mom for a ride. Like her attendance, the quality of her schoolwork is hit-or-miss. When she turns in work and actively participates, she is brilliant, but her inconsistency trips her up. Shelly lives with her mom and younger sister. Recently, Shelly's mom kicked out Shelly's dad again, after a night of drinking and arguing. Shelly is a smart, dedicated student, and she manages to roll out of bed every morning even though she lives with chronic exhaustion due to stress, anxiety, and lack of support. Although Shelly is studious, she has a difficult time managing her relationship with her boyfriend. She is dependent on him to meet all of her social needs, because she finds it all but impossible to maintain friendships with girls. Shelly moves through the days trying to manage intense emotions by pretending everything is fine. On the inside, Shelly feels deeply alone, scared, and sad. On the outside, Shelly seems "good if she would just be more consistent."

Adult Experience

As Shelly's teacher, you are expected to ride the wave and somehow balance Shelly's tardiness and low energy with the fact that she is compliant and kind. She does well enough that she doesn't sound any alarms, yet you notice her poor attendance and that she frequently asks to go to the bathroom and stays out of the class for long periods of time. With 32 other students in the class, you realize you have more pressing fires to put out than Shelly.

If you hope to connect with, teach, and support teens who are living with chronic stress, the first step is to compassionately reconnect with your own inner teenager. Figure 1.1 provides some reflection questions to help you remember a little about your own adolescence.

Figure 1.1   Reconnecting With Your Inner Teenager

What do you remember about your emotions as a teenager?

____

____

____

____

____

What do you remember about your relationships?

____

____

____

____

____

What was most important to you during those years?

____

____

____

____

____

What do you remember most about your high school experience?

____

____

____

____

____

Now that you have briefly reconnected with your inner teenager, you most likely recall that it was an intense and unpredictable time in life. As someone who works with teens, you know better than anyone how fun and meaningful or, alternatively, how exhausting and frustrating it can be, depending on the day. It can be challenging to "ride the wave" and balance the need for flexibility and the need for accountability. One of the keys to being a successful educator is to start by meeting students where they are. Approaching your work with compassion and understanding is the first step toward a successful and healthy school.

Foundation for Effective Practice #1: Adolescent Development—My Brain Made Me Do It

Adolescents are unique unto themselves. They are energetic, impulsive, moody, inquisitive, demanding, hilarious, intriguing, and loving. Those of us in contact with them on a regular basis reap the benefits of some of those qualities rubbing off on us. In order to know how to best serve teens, it is important that you explore and understand what forces are at work. In recent years, with the help of technological advancements like MRIs and brain scans, neuroscientists and psychologists can better map and understand the teenage brain. Modern science has helped validate what we know anecdotally, which is that teens:

- are risk-takers,

- are impulsive,

- don't seem to care about consequences,

- don't usually think things through,

- are heavily influenced by peers, and

- are highly emotional.

[Authors' Note: The authors of this book are not neuroscientists, yet we can appreciate the revolutionary work being done. If this topic sparks your curiosity, check out the references at the back of the book for some useful resources on neuropsychology.]

On the biological side of the teenage experience, the brain is under construction in a major way during adolescence. Teenage brains are in a state of flux. Some parts are growing rapidly; others, more slowly; and some are dormant. Figure 1.2 was adapted from Frances E. Jensen and Amy Ellis Nutt's brain science work *The Teenage Brain* (2016). It is a quick reference for some of the major changes that explain what you see every day in the classroom.

Figure 1.2   The What and the Why of the Teenage Brain

The What	The Why	Classroom Considerations
Teens are moody and overly emotional.	It is not that teens are full of raging hormones but that they are being exposed to certain hormones for the first time, so they are "new" to them and often unsure how to react/respond (p. 20).	Anticipate the emotional roller coaster by not taking it personally. Empathize with variability by being flexible.
They are impulsive.	They lack the ability to inhibit their behavior, because their frontal lobe, which is responsible for executive functioning, is not strongly wired to the rest of the brain yet. It's there, just loosely connected (p. 37).	Patiently repeat, repeat, and repeat again, whether expectations or instructions.
They are risk-takers who don't care about consequences.	It is not the perception of risk, but the anticipation of the reward *despite* the risk, that is stronger in adolescents (Jensen, p. 107). Risk-taking is also an important developmental process that acts as a precursor to decision-making skills as an adult.	Make choices and consequences clear in both procedures and content.
They can't effectively multitask and often forget to do things you've asked.	*Prospective memory*, which is responsible for your ability to hold a task in your mind to do later, is associated with the frontal lobe and is developed strongly from ages 6 to 10—and then not again until the early 20s (p. 40).	Give clear instructions for tasks, making sure to write down steps for successful completion. Be careful not to lay instruction upon instruction at one given time.
Teens are stressed out a lot.	Researchers have shown that, in adolescent rats, the stress response takes up to 3 weeks to calm down, compared to 10 days in adult rats. This indicates that the effects of stress are delayed and possibly irreversible. During times of stress, thinking becomes less flexible (p. 175).	Be calm, consistent, measured, and kind. Combat student stress by not exhibiting stress yourself.

Source: Adapted from Jensen and Nutt (2016).

As if moving through adolescence isn't hard enough on the developing brain, when the effects of chronic stress are introduced, the picture changes even more. For young children who have experienced and/or continue to live in stress-filled environments, the impact on brain development is real. Following are a few symptoms of an unhealthy or underdeveloped brain:

▶ Struggling to remember or memorize things

▶ Difficulty focusing in class or on homework

▶ Not connecting dots between actions and consequences

▶ Inability to control impulses (more so than the average adolescent)

▶ Intense emotional reactions

If you find yourself feeling discouraged or wondering how successful teaching and learning is possible, don't despair. The good news is that the human brain is remarkable in its plasticity and ability to form new neural pathways. That is why consistency, repetition, and corrective emotional experiences are so important to creating new pathways that get reinforced over time. The ability to heal, learn, and grow always exists, and change is possible.

Foundation for Effective Practice #2: Identity Formation—*Who Am I?*

On the psychological side, adolescence—as a life stage—ends at around 24 years old and is a crucial step toward becoming a healthy, functioning adult. One of the primary developmental tasks of this life stage is *identity formation*. Identity formation is all about figuring out who you are, so it is no wonder that teens become hyper-focused on peers as a way of gathering data about what others are doing in relationship to their own self. Social norms, expectations, fitting in, and individuating at the same time are all paramount to figuring out where your edges are.

This is why peer relationships are so important. Like bats, which use echolocation to find their way in the dark, teens send out social signals to each other about what is cool, how to act, what belonging means, and other cues to help form their individual selves. Adolescents are hyper-focused on peers to help inform, develop, and explore social norms around school life, dating, limit setting, sex, boundaries . . . everything. Teens are watching, testing, practicing, and copying each other in order to figure it all out.

Foundation for Effective Practice #3: Risk-Taking and Psychological Safety

Mr. Bennett is in the middle of a history lesson when he poses a question to the class. Instead of answering the question, George responds with, "Hey Mr. B, why are your pants so tight?!" The whole class erupts in laughter. Mr. Bennett stands there for a moment, shocked and embarrassed, then simply writes George a detention and quietly hands it to him. George grabs it like it's a first-place trophy and heads to the dean's office.

Risk-Taking

You may find yourself thinking, *Why would George do that, knowing that kind of behavior will get him kicked out of class?* One possibility is that the *reward* of the laughter and approval from his classmates, plus the shot of dopamine that hits the pleasure center of his brain, *outweighs the consequence* of the referral. It isn't that he doesn't care about the punishment so much as he cares more about the reward (Jensen & Nutt, 2016).

When you're a developing person, risk-taking is an important step in figuring out where your edges are. *What are my limits? Where can I stretch and grow? How much is too much? Who am I?* Although these questions are at the heart of identity formation, they may also be capitalized on by teachers for effective student engagement. We know that teens are wired to take risks because of the anticipation of reward, often regardless of consequences, and we know that they are highly social, so the question becomes "How do you maximize the risk/reward and capitalize on positive peer pressure in ways that are appropriate and helpful in the classroom?" As a teacher, you want to think of ways to maximize the risk-taking mechanism that is already built in to your students. How do you talk about what risky behaviors are okay, even encouraged, in your classroom? How might you make risk-taking a high-reward exercise?

Psychological Safety

Positive risk-taking in the classroom is challenging for teens, because they are so connected in their social networks; it can feel like a big risk to speak up in class, ask for clarification, or admit they don't know something. They are sensitive to being ridiculed or seen in an unfavorable light by their peers. This is where psychological safety comes in. Psychological safety is broadly defined as a climate in which people are comfortable expressing and being themselves. More specifically, when people have psychological safety, they feel comfortable sharing concerns, and they can make mistakes without fear of embarrassment or retribution. They can speak up and won't be humiliated, ignored, or blamed (Edmondson, 2019). Students with chronic stress and trauma need psychological safety as much as physical safety in order to learn, take risks, and grow.

You may have all the right structures in place so that kids feel safe to ask a question, say the wrong answer, talk to you about an assignment they don't understand, or ask for help—and yet they don't. It can be super frustrating. Figure 1.3 provides some reflection questions to help you increase your awareness of psychological safety.

Figure 1.3   Creating Psychological Safety in Your Classroom

1. Have I clearly named my expectations and what students can expect from me?
2. How do I initiate a conversation, extend a hand for students to walk through the door, or simply just check in (instead of assuming they will if they need to)?
3. How am I role-modeling psychological safety by being vulnerable and transparent (while staying in my role)?
4. Have I created a safe space for students to take risks, such as asking a question in front of the class (knowing they are afraid of being laughed at by their peers)?

What Works in the Classroom: Adolescent-Centered Teaching and Learning

You've made the choice to spend your days with teenagers. Who does that? This is essentially the question Brooke's father posed after she informed him that she was not going to be pursuing an MBA; rather, she was going back to school to become a teacher. She made this choice because she connected the importance of education with a free and civil society, and she wanted to be part of something that mattered: teaching and learning. Plus, she had watched enough *Law & Order* to know that a jury consisted of average people who needed to be able to critically think and evaluate. Fostering thinkers was an important ideal. This was not the only draw for Brooke. She was captivated by the energy, creativity, and outright hilarity of working with adolescents.

Fast-forward several decades, and Brooke is still fascinated by students in this stage of development. Daily, their fearless imaginations aim to make sense of the opposing forces in the world: good versus evil, justice versus oppression, freedom versus obligation, fun versus boring, individuality versus belonging. Adolescents continue the quest for social connection, ownership, and meaning in an increasingly complex and stressful world. As a teacher, how can you harness this amazing time of life while addressing the specific needs of those students who have experienced chronic stress and trauma and/or continue to do so?

Meaningful Connections in Learning Communities

You're sitting at your desk, ready to start the class. The bell rings, but no one seems to notice. Clusters of students are standing around all talking at once, arms around one another, leaning in close to glean a morsel of gossip. Laughter erupts as one student cracks a joke. Another in the group glances around to see if someone else has heard. They are fully engaged with one another and totally oblivious to the fact the class has begun. It is not until you ask them to take their seats that they begin to peel apart, but not until one last hug is exchanged and one last secret shared.

As the teacher, what now? How can you capitalize on what adolescents need at this stage of their development, particularly promoting their need for voice and choice?

Be Not Afraid

As class begins, the power of community is unleashed. Let's face it, most students come to school because of the social scene. This may initially come as a blow to those of us who entered the teaching field with the primary goal of sharing our passion for a particular field of study, like literature or chemistry. We view our work, as middle- or high school teachers, through the content lens, rather than the kid lens—as opposed to our elementary counterparts. We don't receive much pre-service education about adolescent development and teenagers' relational nature—and certainly not much, if any, regarding the impacts of adverse childhood experiences and chronic stress. However, over time, we begin to learn that an essential part of teaching teenagers is about harnessing, directing, and channeling our students' social energy—not trying to extinguish or ignore it. The result gives way to experiencing joy in teaching and engagement in learning, both outcomes that inspired us to do this work in the first place.

Honestly speaking, adolescent energy can be intimidating. Teachers fear that students may take over the class and that things may get out of control. So, the typical response is to create more order by placing students in rows, isolating them from one another, reinforcing the "rules," lecturing, having them fill out worksheets, dictating, and essentially squelching the revolt. This is a misguided approach. If you learn to tactically direct students' need for connection, and the energy that accompanies it, then you have an opportunity for robust learning environments whereby you capitalize on what is before you. In fact, research tells us that learning is a social endeavor (Vygotsky, 1978). By taking advantage of this psycho-neurological fact, you will be able to work with the forces of nature rather than battle something that could make your classroom more effective and fun for everyone.

In addition to energy, humor, drama, and fun, connection brings with it a protective factor against stress and harm. Longitudinal studies that follow students who have experienced adverse childhood events, like those conducted by Charisse Nixon, point to the critical importance of connection and the meaningfulness of it. In fact, the children who are most resilient despite having experienced trauma are those who have a meaningful connection to an adult (non-parent included) (Nixon, 2016). As we translate this research to the classroom, it becomes evident that there is ample opportunity for teachers to design environments in which they are leaders in connection and intentionally create an atmosphere that is ripe for meaningful relationships.

> **Promoting *student voice/choice*:**
>
> - Every student seeks to be known as an individual.
> - Every student desires to have connection—even if they disguise that desire.
> - Every student is trying to find his or her voice.

Foster Identity

The social construct of community exists to meet our basic needs: to belong, to be protected, to feel valued, and to share—essentially, to avoid ostracism (Ren, Wesselmann, & Williams, 2018). Other social constructs, such as families, teams, platoons, crews, and clubs, function to meet similar human needs. In the animal kingdom, gaggles, coveys, bales, colonies, parliaments, and troops exist to guarantee survival at the most basic level. As natural as inclusion is to humans, a unique aspect of adolescent development places an increased emphasis on being an individual—set apart for being "myself"—yet within a group. In a classroom, these forces play out in how the teacher designs a "learning" community. There are several considerations for both building a community and, simultaneously, establishing ways for each individual student to add his or her unique contribution. In a classroom, it's a balance between *Me* and *Us*.

As a starting point, invite students to identify who they are and to identify that which makes them different . . . and the same. Take, for example, Mr. Marshall's practice. Mr. Marshall asks students in each of his classes to come up with an object or metaphor that illustrates who they are as a learning community, yet accentuates each of them as individuals. Over the years, students have come up with mosaics, woven fabrics, puzzles, constellations, and quilts. This year, he is using a quilt to demonstrate how no two people (pieces) are identical and the way in which all the pieces, together, make something beautiful. He encourages students to select fabric that speaks to them as individuals, including their origin and cultural representation. His students from Ghana particularly value adding African tribal fabrics to the design, as do his students who feel most represented by batik from southeast Asia. Mr. Marshall adds his own representative piece to every collective, because he is an equal member of the community. He is not afraid to belong. His belonging does not translate to letting students operate without boundaries or to his relinquishing control. Rather, it signals that individual membership matters, as does each person in the room, and that it is not *Me (Teacher) versus Them (Students)*. This class work product reflects the importance of the parts that constitute a whole. A symbol like his serves to buoy the community as the school year wears on, fatigue sets in, and anxiety rises; it serves to remind *us* that *we are not alone*; we are part of something larger and lovelier.

Can you think of a symbol, object, or metaphor that might embody both the individual and the collective within your content area and interest?

Promoting *student voice/choice*:

- Every student has a unique contribution to make to the community.
- Every student desires to be seen and heard.
- Every student wants to be genuinely loved for himself or herself.

Maximize Social Dynamics in Learning

To elevate student engagement, as discussed previously, you need to capitalize on the social aspect of your students, in addition to providing means for them to focus on their individual thinking, understanding, and contribution. In doing so, your planning practices should focus on implementing multiple ways for students to work individually, in small groups, and as a whole group within your community. Underlying these varying formats are several premises:

- Student thinking is paramount.

- Students need multiple opportunities to construct meaning— individually and socially.

- Student learning is an active process.

Therefore, they must be at the center of the activities, within each format. Flexibility and adaptability are key. For instance, written responses may be best addressed individually first—giving students time to organize their thinking—followed by sharing in small groups. Students have difficult days, so use your judgment in allowing students more individual time when it looks as if they need a moment to regroup. If small-group work is the main instructional format, then encouraging students to participate may be the best path to engagement. Knowing students is foundational to matching them as individuals to the best learning process. Figure 1.4 illustrates the planning needed to match learning goals with learning formats.

Figure 1.4   Formats for Social Learning

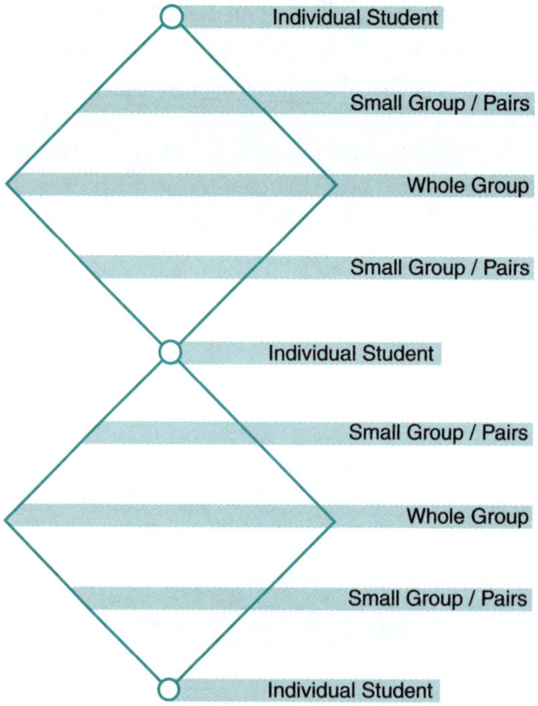

❑ *At the **Individual level:** I (the student) have the opportunity to . . . check in with my thinking about the topic.*

❑ *At the **Small Group/Pairs level:** I (the student) have the opportunity to . . . lean in with my peers to share my thinking and to hear their thinking. The possibility of generating "our" thinking exists.*

❑ *At the **Whole Group level:** I (the student) have the opportunity to . . . hear from my peers about their thinking and identify "our" thinking about the topic.*

Source: Figure layout by Bill Grimmer.

Promoting *student voice/choice*:

- Each student's thinking is as unique as his or her fingerprints and DNA.
- Students contribute their work individually, in small groups/pairs, and in whole group as a means of learning.
- Students can indicate with whom they'd like to work or when they need a reprieve.

Shared Ownership: Owning What We Create

Alana, like most kids her age, is highly aware of her surroundings. When she enters the biology classroom, she quickly scans the room, looking for her friends and the connection they provide. As Ms. Booker, her biology teacher, welcomes her, she replies without making eye contact, "Hey, Miss!" She is most interested in settling into her spot, locating her friends, and getting comfortable.

The Importance of Place

Although technically Room 414 is Ms. Booker's classroom, it is a space shared by both the teacher and the students. The room is home to science equipment, posters, and lab stations. Ms. Booker has made this learning space her own. It feels like science should be happening here.

Similarly, students seek to make their learning spaces their own, as well. Ever notice how they move chairs, place their backpacks, write on their desks, litter the floor, sit near their friends, pick a spot in the back, and slouch in their chairs? It is fascinating to watch students accommodate themselves as best they can in learning spaces that are static and rigid in nature. This speaks to their need to find their own place. As a teacher, you must decide what strategy to use in order to help students create a comfortable, safe place. We address the concept of safety later in this book, yet it is worth mentioning here also, because adolescents, particularly students affected by trauma and stress, seek to be safe in both a physical and an emotional sense. Their specific vulnerability lies in this stage of development, where the executive functioning aspect of the brain does not yet override the "lizard" part of the brain (Siegel & Bryson, 2011), the evolutionarily primitive part that initiates the "fight, flight, or freeze" response to perceived dangers. Helping adolescents feel "at home" in the classroom frees up their energy and focus to learn the subject at hand. To this end, offering options as to where and with whom to sit empowers students to make choices that they see as serving their best interest. With your input as necessary, this small but important aspect of control of the learning environment will help anchor the adolescent learner.

The Importance of Materials

"Is there one more for me?" "Are there enough?" Teachers hear these questions frequently, in both subtle and loud ways. Students seeking access to a laptop, a copy of the text, markers, sticky notes, a calculator, a microscope, or a better view of the board tend to either ask outright or withdraw. The cost of not providing each student access to the materials is distraction or a missed opportunity to grapple with the content. Many students may look engaged, but how do you know if they cannot annotate, highlight, underline, or use sticky notes to record their thinking? Ensuring that each student has a copy of the text, for example, increases the likelihood that he or she will have the opportunity to read and interact with the material, ultimately increasing understanding. This is particularly true as you aim to create more active and hands-on activities. Planning for *all hands* is a critical aspect in promoting ownership of not only the materials, but of the intended educational experience.

Caring for Place and Materials

As you strive to provide places and materials that foster belonging and ownership, consider teaching your students to care for both elements of the classroom. Given that they may be perceived as irresponsible or careless—when in fact and more accurately, they are developmentally prone to appear as such—it is important to explicitly teach them to care for the place and materials they encounter. This is particularly helpful for students whose home environments and norms are inconsistent with those of the school. Eliminating assumptions that students should know what to do helps all members of the learning community be successful. Recall that a number of students who come from chaotic environments don't automatically know the norms. Be clear: Your job is to create an organized and comfortable learning environment and to provide pertinent learning materials. Their job is to be responsible for maintaining a clean classroom and ensuring that materials are in good repair. Build time into each class period in order to accommodate this aspect of shared ownership. For example, a teacher we know routinely smiles and has students "push in chairs, collect three pieces of garbage, and say thanks to a peer as you exit." Simple, direct, and caring.

Promoting *student voice/choice*:

- Students need to be comfortable in their place—that is, in the seating arrangement and their location.
- Students need to "own" their materials. Each student has a copy or access.
- Students care for their classroom environment and materials and are encouraged to do so.

Co-owning Process/Procedure

As we bring Alana back into the picture and recognize Ms. Booker's attention to providing her ownership of her place and materials, let's examine the importance of naming the role of both teacher and students in order to amplify shared ownership. In the first weeks of school, Ms. Booker provides the following information to students: "The Basics of How We Roll in Ms. Booker's Classroom" (Figure 1.5).

Ms. Booker offers students an opportunity to offer their opinions about her listing. She makes modifications as students share their ideas—not all will work in a classroom setting; even so, she strives to add as much student voice as is feasible. It's important to her that her students see themselves in how the classroom operates.

Figure 1.5 The Basics of How We Roll in Ms. Booker's Classroom

As the teacher, I will . . .	As the student, you will . . .
• Be respectful of you as an individual. • Be aware of your need to own your learning. • Be prepared. • Be fair. • Provide you guidance in your learning.	• Be respectful of yourself and others. • Be prepared to meet the demands of this learning environment. • Advocate for yourself to be your best self. • Know that you have options. • Be engaged. • Take care of this place and your materials.

When we step out of our roles by not following through, then . . .

- I will give you a verbal heads-up. You may give me a heads-up also.
- I will give you a second verbal heads-up. You can give me one too.
- We will check in by having a one-on-one conversation outside of class in order to problem solve.
- We may need to bring in outside support, such as a parent, family member, school counselor, dean, or assistant principal.
- We will identify a plan that helps both of us maintain our roles in this learning community.

As the school year moves forward, Ms. Booker allocates time for students to reflect on their roles and her role. This looks like a simple half-sheet of paper with two columns, including plus and delta sign. Students share their experience with what is going well and what could use refinement. Ms. Booker considers the feedback and circles back as a class with improvements. See the following example of a student response from the end of the first quarter:

As a student	As the teacher
+ I participate regularly in classroom discussion.	+ You make learning fun.
+ I do my homework.	+ You are organized.
Δ Sometimes, when I am confused, I don't ask for help.	Δ Sometimes I need more help with understanding when I get confused.

In another example, at the beginning of each school year Mr. Gluck, a middle school math teacher, asks students to name what they think makes them their best selves in math class. He invites students to take risks in naming for themselves what works, rather than regurgitating what they think he wants to hear. What you see in Figure 1.6 reflects each student's input as he or she individually makes sense of what he or she needs to show up in a manner that fosters success. Note that the poster is in student language; it's not a purchased poster with canned statements. Students love to see their own words!

Figure 1.6 Mr. Gluck's Math Class

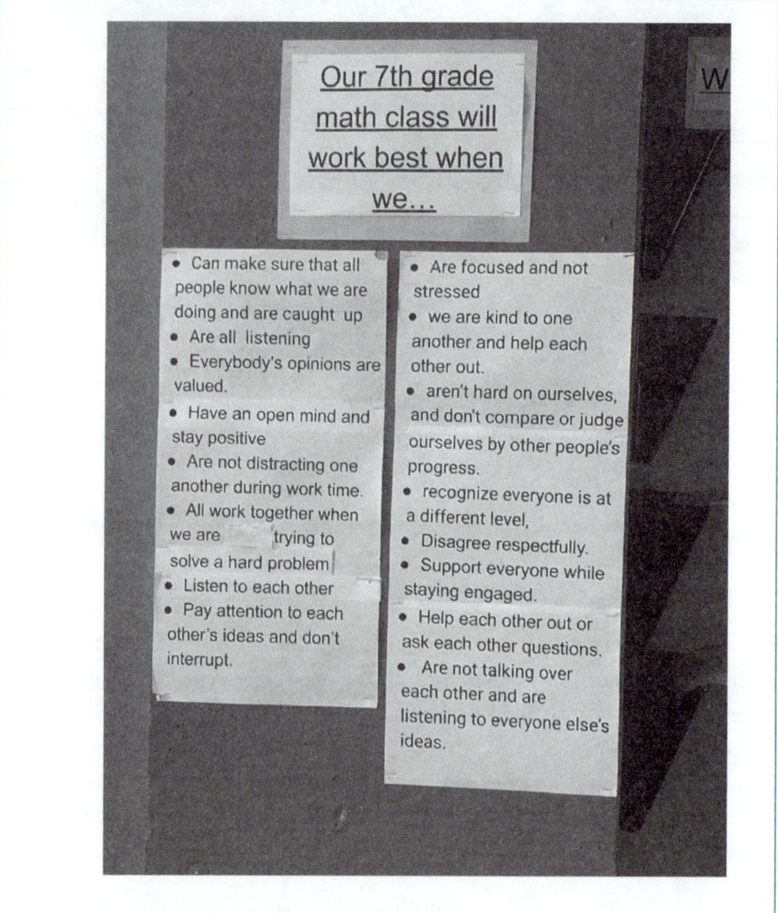

Source: Created by Art Gluck and his students.

Promoting *student voice/choice*:

- Students have clarity about the roles of the teacher and the student, as well as the process of maintaining those roles.
- Students take risks to share their ideas and opinions about what works for them individually.
- Students are asked to continually provide feedback related to classroom process and procedures.

The Purpose of Learning

Not surprisingly, students wonder why school matters. In fact, all learners, no matter their age, seek to find meaning in their education. Who among us doesn't seek purpose in what we do? As general education vies for importance and relevance in an ever-changing society, the classroom is faced with the challenge of meeting students' needs through content selection, student inquiry, assessment, and risk-taking. These components may sound like nothing new; however, in response to the turbulent world that surrounds adolescents, there is a call to make school more meaningful and relevant to their young lives. For students with a history of trauma, in particular, having meaning in school can be a source of comfort—a reprieve from chaos.

Content Selections

As you seek to foster student ownership, providing students opportunity to pick the topics that they study can unlock their motivation. As in adult life, we seek out that which sparks our interest and connects to our lives. When we're asked to pursue topics of little to no interest, our motivation wanes. Think of the last obligatory task that you were asked to perform, say attending an in-service in which the topic was irrelevant or showing up for jury duty when you felt you hadn't the time to spare. These experiences force us to identify our own purposes, like wanting to keep a job or avoid a warrant for arrest. To students, pursuing their own topics of interest seems less burdensome and more like an opportunity.

In a recent social studies class where students were reading *I Am Malala*—the best-selling memoir by Nobel Prize–winner Malala Yousafzai, who grew up in a Taliban-controlled region of Pakistan—they were asked what they wondered about given their varying degree of background knowledge about the author, the Taliban, Islam, and Pakistan. After individually jotting down as much as possible and talking briefly at their tables, students reported out the working knowledge they had about the topic. The teacher, Mr. Peters, while working within this required text within the curriculum unit, filled up the whiteboard with each group's responses. It was packed with all kinds of connections, like Middle East relations, the Quran, women's education, extremism, human rights, and the Nobel Peace Prize. There was a lot there to study within a five-to-six-week unit.

Mr. Peters asked students to vote on which topics were they the most interested in learning more about. The three that surfaced were extremism, human rights, and the Quran. As a result, Mr. Peters supplemented the anchor text with a variety of journalistic articles, film, art pieces, and primary sources. Certainly, as the teacher, he had to curate all the materials that were available and determine what was most important given the time constraints. Students helped with this process by offering up sources they were able to locate while researching on their own. Mr. Peters was deliberate about being sure that students were able to offer up their selections, and he encouraged them to pursue additional reading and watching outside of class. He knew that they couldn't possibly uncover all that his students were wondering about; however, this was a solid start. Most important, students were able to follow their own curiosity about a given topic in light of a stated curriculum scope and sequence, which is most common in schools.

Criteria for Success

As you continue to provide a place for students to connect with their own learning and thereby create ownership, it's important to highlight the role of assessment and knowing what skills, knowledge, and dispositions will contribute to success. Connie Moss and Susan Brookhart, in their book *Learning Targets* (2012), address this practice by insisting that teachers clarify for students and with students those attributes that constitute accurate demonstration of a particular task—for example, students use a listing of criteria for success prior to preparing a presentation, in order to guarantee the greatest likelihood of meeting expectations. In the absence of stated expectations, students must play the game of *Guess What the Teacher Is Thinking*. In this dynamic, instead of homing in on what constitutes a shared successful demonstration of learning, students focus on what they perceive will meet with the teacher's personal approval. Some perceptions are more accurate than others, but all are subjective. This is dicey for students, as it creates a nebulous understanding of both the task and the teacher's expectations, as well as an increased possibility of misunderstanding the topic—all of which increase student stress.

As we spoke about earlier in this chapter, the adolescent brain is not wired to function most effectively around task breakdown and completion—the executive-functioning aspect of cognition. This aspect of learning is further complicated by the neurological effects of chronic stress and trauma, which may impair functioning. You will assist your students greatly when you use criteria for success—clarity—and direct their attention to that which matters most in completing the work. The clearer the target, the greater the chance of success in hitting it.

Promoting *student voice/choice*:

- Student curiosity has a role in curriculum.
- Students need an opportunity to select resources that inform their understanding.
- Students need to know what specifically constitutes success.

Meaningful Curriculum Design

Above, we briefly touched upon the role of students in curriculum design. This section directly addresses three important considerations for drawing students into their learning through curriculum by addressing three critical attributes of impact, relevance, and methodology.

Impact: What Difference Does This Make?

When you think of impact, consider the vast number of students who enter your classroom unsure of what they are doing there, aside from it being mandatory that they attend according to their class schedules and perhaps the law. In fact, a student may remind you that he has to be in school until the age of 16, and then he "is going to do something that he really likes." When asked to expand on what he likes, he may reply, "You know, the stuff I care about, like getting a job and having freedom." Your task as a teacher may be to help adolescents see the purpose not only of a particular subject but perhaps also of school in general. Certainly you aim for them to see that a specific subject, task, or class will prepare them for college or life. It can be a stretch, however, to offer students a vision of the lifetime benefits of a formal education when getting through the day is sometimes all that is in view. This is all the more reason to plan your curriculum cognizant of the difference the learning really makes. You must be brave enough to continually ask yourself, *Who cares?* If you can't answer this, then consider shifting the direction or exploring what contexts might make this learning matter to an adolescent.

In addition to anchoring the work with impact in mind, consider that students seek to know that they can make a difference. This belief, loosely referred to as student efficacy, drives students forward with the sense that the work they do in school matters in the real world. Adolescents, in particular, have a strong need for self-efficacy in making change in their world, whether at school, at home, or in the community at large. Plus, it helps students who experience little control in other areas of their lives to develop a sense that their actions do have an impact. What you ask them to do each day can either encourage this desire to impact their worlds or tamp it down.

Finally, learners ask themselves, *Who is listening to me, and do they care?* Assuming that their work is for the teacher's eyes only limits the imagined impact it can have. Writing an opinion piece, for instance, with your teacher as the only audience is not as motivating as writing the same piece for a blog, newspaper, or newsletter. Most state standards for literacy work stipulate the importance of broadening audience, as well as considering publication and dissemination (U.S. Department of Education, 2019). We'd all like to see our work "in print" and shared with others, particularly if it feels important to us.

Relevance: Who Does This in the Real World?

Chances are, if your students can identify where in the real world the work exists, it will lead them to examine who does this kind of work. For example, learning about artists, journalists, YouTubers, architects, social workers, gamers, and actors will connect students to applications outside the classroom. This is important to adolescent learners, because identifying those adults who do what interests them peels back the layers of preconceived notions of what it takes to develop similar skills and knowledge base. There is the possibility, they realize, to become like those they admire. Close examination of the people who are doing what students care about leads them to gain access by apprenticing the practices and strategies that help these folks make an impact. Students are able to pull back the curtain and see the effort that is behind the perception.

Methodology: How Do I Do This Work?

For starters, students need to take risks. The adolescent brain strives to take risks; it seeks to do so. To maximize this reality, curriculum offers great possibility for each student to take risks in his or her learning by making hypotheses, trying a new approach, demonstrating learning through an alternative modality, or venturing into the unknown.

Learning is messy, and the sooner you offer students this acknowledgment, the better. If you can help students pursue topics and answer questions that don't have a clear-cut solution or one right answer, the better. Not only is this more strategic in working with the adolescent penchant for learning, but it more closely mirrors the real world. Adults know that nothing is ever as easy as it seems. Frankly, we also know that we deal with complex issues and day-to-day messiness more than we deal with the straightforward and clear-cut. We can assist young learners to address the truth that learning is an endeavor laced with uncertainty and risk of being wrong. This is not a mortal flaw; it's reality, and the work of school should prepare students for precisely that—reality.

In grappling with the uncertainty and messiness, adolescents need focus. Multitasking is inefficient and often counterproductive. Asking students to think of a variety of topics at once, or peppering them with questions and tasks simultaneously, prevents them (and you, as the teacher) from gaining ground. In the classroom context, giving instructions one at a time with written support is helpful, as is having students record the steps they think are needed to complete a particular task, such as solving word problems, approaching a science lab, or writing a summary (Siegel, 2013).

Ted Sizer, a thought leader and educator in secondary education, said:

> My basic conclusion is contained in the aphorism "Less is more." I believe that the qualities of mind that should be the goal of high school need time to grow and that they develop best when engaging a few, important ideas deeply. (Sizer, 2004, p. 89)

We couldn't agree more. The task of curriculum and instruction is not to inundate students with more information and a variety of tasks, but to have them think deeply about fewer and more meaningful topics.

They can "Google" most questions and find simplistic answers. In fact, information is abundant, yet thoughtful and complex thinking is not. The work of meaningful learning is slow, messy, and in need of great attention to young people who seek impact, relevance, and know-how. Your classroom can provide all of these attributes, if you are willing to seek these as well in your own practices through thoughtful curriculum design. Figure 1.7 helps further define how to design meaningful curriculum in order to best serve the adolescent learner.

Figure 1.7   Designing Meaningful Curriculum

Meaningful Curriculum Seeks . . .	Meaningful Curriculum Avoids . . .
Depth	Low-level activity (i.e., I can locate it on Google)
Creative input	Pedantic approaches
Fearlessness	Timidity
Messy methods	Rote methods
A broad purpose for learning	Limited purpose (i.e., this lives only in the classroom or academia)
A broad audience	Limited audience (i.e., my teacher is the only one who assesses it)
Complex solutions (i.e., there is more than one right answer)	Simple solutions or silver bullets
Multiple methods to finding the solution (i.e., there is more than one way to find the answer)	Kill and drill
The greater good	Egotism (this is all about you and your gain)
Individual accountability	Free-riding
Focusing	Multitasking
Collaboration	Isolation
Students doing the "work"	Teacher doing the "work"

Promoting *student voice/choice*:

- Students want to know that their learning makes a difference.
- Students want to know that they can individually make a difference.
- Students want to take risks in their learning.

Taking Understanding School-Wide

Teaching adolescents is a great joy . . . and a tremendous undertaking. They are a special group of students, capable of incredible thought and action. If you are a school leader, you have an obligation to make the most of this powerful time in human development.

Keeping the Kids in Focus

Provide direct instruction about adolescent development, including case studies and role-plays that highlight the inherent joys, complexities, and possibilities of adolescent education. Educate faculty and staff on the effects of adverse childhood experiences (ACEs) on student learning and behavior. Several schools that we know of have a team of teachers and counselors who regularly present to the whole school community about the adolescent learner and ACEs. They showcase student experience throughout particularly stressful times of high school, such as the first weeks of freshman year, exam periods, college applications, grade reports, holidays, and the second semester of senior year. By bringing the student experience into close examination, teachers can anticipate and plan for how to best support students and prepare themselves to take on the additional stress that students bring with them during these seasons. Success is in the planning. The more teachers know what their students are experiencing, the better they can incorporate into their curriculum, instruction, and assessment high-leverage practices that increase connection and ownership.

School-Wide Curricular Focus on What Matters to Adolescents

Make high-school diplomas represent a compendium of study that prepares students for college, postsecondary options, and real-world application. While fulfilling seat time, demand that curriculum provide students with high-interest and varied texts, real-world learning experiences, and meaning beyond the classroom. It's not enough for students to complete worksheets and listen to lectures. They need to have opportunity after opportunity to apply their understanding and stretch themselves to gain skills that will serve them well long after they walk across the graduation stage. Give teachers license to take their own risks in designing learning experiences that draw in the adolescent learner through relevance and meaningful work. Provide teachers options to attend conferences, design curriculum together, study effective practices in adolescent learning, and wrestle with new practices that increase buy-in from students. Make an intentional decision to invest in teachers by encouraging avenues for growth and renewal that pertain specifically to the adolescent learner. Finally, ask students what they both want and need to learn in order to navigate their increasingly complex worlds.

Reflections

Working with teenagers is messy, delightful, challenging work. Don't be afraid of their powerful energy. Lean into it. Thinking of ways to harness the energy and work within the limitations of the student's developmental life stage will actually make your job easier and fun!

1. What do I love about working with teenagers?

2. What am I curious about?

3. What makes me nervous about working with teenagers?

4. What feels possible?

Toolkit for Tomorrow

In an effort to cultivate connection, tomorrow I can:

- ❑ understand adolescent development, trauma, and chronic stress as it relates to teaching and learning.
- ❑ be aware of how I might react to students who are acting out (i.e., being normal teens).
- ❑ identify a plan for the unexpected.
- ❑ identify a plan for how time is going to be used.
- ❑ be curious and flexible.
- ❑ ride the wave versus get triggered by adolescent behavior.
- ❑ share with students clear expectations for risk-taking.
- ❑ share with students clear expectations for peer-to-peer interactions.
- ❑ ask a colleague for insight or collaboration. (I am not alone.)
- ❑ get support from my coach or administrator or from the school counselor.
- ❑ lead with compassion . . . for myself and others.

In the End, Be Loving

Joyful teaching results from embracing adolescent learners for who they are. It results from meeting the needs of students who suffer from life's circumstances beyond our classrooms. The wackiness, unpredictability, and dynamic nature of teenagers is the great joy of our work. Cherish the successes and the struggles! Your presence in your students' lives makes a difference!

Self-Regulation Is the Key to Calm

Smile, breathe and go slowly.
—**Thich Nhat Hanh**

Thursday morning, 5:30 a.m. It's dark. And cold. You lie in bed staring at the ceiling, thinking about the day ahead and taking inventory of the events to come. Period by period. And then it hits you. *Third period. Jamie.* You feel a wave of dread wash over you, and you think, *Maybe he'll be absent and I won't have to deal with him today.*

Your thoughts return to what happened yesterday when he heckled you during your lecture until finally you yelled at him and gave him a detention, after which he stormed out, leaving you feeling angry and out of control. You wondered how things escalated so quickly, while you tried to get the class back on track for the remainder of the period.

Although you are the teacher, Jamie is the ringleader. Jamie sets the tone. From the minute he strolls in late, commanding the attention of the students who were on task, the disruption begins. What will it be that sets him off today? The most frustrating thing about him is that when he is "good," he is so great. He shows real leadership potential, he is super bright, and he's actually pretty funny. But man, when he is "off," he can drag you and your classroom down! So here you are, 5:36 a.m., and you already find yourself circling the drain.

Self-Regulation: Why Is It Important?

Chronic stress is an epidemic in today's schools—in urban, suburban, and rural schools, regardless of students' socioeconomic status. Self-regulation and being a force for helping others regulate is key to combating the stress that you and your students are both experiencing. Understanding dysregulation is important, because dysregulated teachers cannot teach and dysregulated students cannot learn. The ideas put forth in this chapter are meant to support *you,* so that you can best support your dysregulated students. We invite you to read it with an open mind and heart, knowing that your greatest strength will be to create awareness of your own reactions and symptoms of dysregulation. This chapter will focus on exploring the concept of regulation, in simple terms, as a means of staying grounded and calm when you encounter a student, an adult, or a system that is dysregulated, so that you can be more effective.

Dysregulated people can have an overloaded or underloaded nervous system. This can happen when we experience a lack of safety, protection, and predictable environments. Children and adolescents are especially vulnerable to dysregulation, because they are still developing physically, psychologically, and emotionally. Remember, adolescence doesn't end until a person is in his or her mid-twenties. When encountering unrelenting stress at any age, knowing how to bring yourself back from chaos to calm requires awareness, the ability to manage your environment, and coping skills.

Student Experience

Jamie is a great example of how one student's dysregulation can take down a whole classroom environment. Energy is powerful. How is it that one student can shift the momentum of the entire class? Jamie already has his teacher consumed with dread before he is even out of bed. That should be a clue that things are out of balance.

Jamie's own dysregulated system was expressed by his impulsive and aggressive behavior. He was not able to be calm or de-escalate. He was amped up, he triggered the teacher to be reactive, and things escalated quickly.

If the teacher, as the adult, feels the power of Jamie's dysregulation so intensely, imagine the impact on Jamie's classmates. Things can go south so quickly. Students who have experienced chronic stress and trauma are quickly triggered and derailed when a situation escalates, as it did with Jamie. Students, consciously and subconsciously, are looking to their teacher to keep the class in a balanced state, to maintain a sense of calm so that learning can continue.

Adult Experience

When experiencing dysregulation, it is easy to resort to the old standbys: referring the student to the office, engaging in a power struggle with the student, yelling, or shaming. However, the first step in de-escalating situations like the one with Jamie is to create awareness about your own reaction, while simultaneously imagining the student's response as well. Figure 2.1 lists some physiological, emotional, and cognitive events that both you and the student might experience when things blow up.

What do you notice about these descriptions? Yes, they are the same. Whenever a person *feels* threatened—under attack, shamed, insecure,

Figure 2.1 What Escalating Conflict Feels Like for You and Your Students

Event	Student Experience	Your Experience
Physiological	• Increased heart rate • Change in body temperature • Sweat • Shaking • Brain shuts down • Panic	• Increased heart rate • Change in body temperature • Sweat • Shaking • Brain shuts down • Panic
Emotional	• Anger/rage • Embarrassment • Defensiveness (survival/saving • face) • Aggressiveness (survival/saving face)	• Anger/rage • Embarrassment • Defensiveness (survival/saving • face) • Aggressiveness (survival/saving face)
Cognitive	• *He hates me.* • *This isn't fair.* • *I am stupid.* • *People are laughing at me.* • *I have been disrespected.* • *I hate him.* • *He doesn't listen to me.* • *He doesn't care.*	• *He hates me.* • *This isn't fair.* • *I suck at my job.* • *People are laughing at me.* • *I have been disrespected.* • *I hate him.* • *He doesn't listen to me.* • *He doesn't care.*

confused, or all of the above—these symptoms follow suit. When we are in relationships with people we value and want to trust, the stakes are even higher, which can create even more distress.

Foundation for Effective Practice #1: Understanding the Body's Reaction to Stress and Dysregulation

Stress and trauma impact us at the most basic and biological levels of functioning—the brain and the nervous system. Changes in brain chemistry can overload the nervous system and negatively impact cognitive functioning, mood, and the ability to learn.

Upstairs Brain/Downstairs Brain

Our human nervous system is one of the most powerful survival mechanisms we have. The autonomic nervous system is an amazing warning system that alerts us to danger. Since the beginning of time, all animals (humans included) have had a built-in alert system that signals when there is danger, so that we can make a split-second decision to fight, flee, or freeze. In his book *The Whole-Brain Child,* psychiatrist and researcher Daniel Siegel (2011) simplified how our brains work by describing two essential parts of the brain:

> Imagine that your brain is a house, with both a downstairs and upstairs. The downstairs brain includes two parts; the brain stem, and the limbic region, which are both located in the lower parts of the brain. Scientists talk about these lower areas as being more primitive because they are responsible for basic functions (like breathing and blinking), for innate reactions and impulses (like fight or flight) and for strong emotions (like anger and fear). . . . Your upstairs brain is completely different, more evolved and can give you a fuller perspective on your world. This is where more intricate mental processes take place like thinking, imagining, and planning. (pp. 38–40)

The lower part of the brain (downstairs brain) is responsible for the "fight, flight, or freeze" response. It is activated when there is *perceived* danger.

This is a really important point, because it isn't just actual danger, but the individual's *perception of danger* that starts the process. Once the process has been triggered, the brain floods the body with adrenaline that gets the heart racing, the mind focuses on a singular task, and the body gets ready for action. In the midst of this reaction, everything disappears into the background so that you can focus all of your resources on survival. For Jamie, once his downstairs brain took over, he couldn't see any other possibility except fight.

The downstairs brain is meant to put a person on high alert, and it shuts down the upstairs brain, which is the part of the brain responsible for executive functioning and decision processing. For example, if you are hiking on a trail and you see a mountain lion up ahead, it is not the time to be wondering what you'll cook for dinner or where you'll spend your next vacation. Instead, your most important thought should be *What do I do now?* You have only a couple of choices. You can fight the mountain lion, you can run from it, or you can freeze where you are (play dead) in hopes that it just moves on.

The "fight, flight, or freeze" response is biological. It is a primal reaction to a perceived fear. It is not personal. It is not malicious. It is not intentional. It is a survival skill of the highest order. When people act or react from a place of primal fear, they are not doing it *to* you—they are doing it *in spite of you.*

This is a hard lesson to remember when a student challenges you in front of the other students, or when you have repeated yourself for what feels like 300 times to a student who can't stay on task, or when you are feeling out of control. This type of dysregulation that shows up in many different ways can be a result of chronic stress and trauma.

Dysregulation and the Classroom

Dysregulation is like being "out of whack" and out of balance in a way that impairs functioning. Think about it: When you are anxious, angry, or sad, don't the simplest tasks sometimes seem insurmountable? Are you able to focus on work when you are experiencing a personal crisis? People, and especially children, who live in chaotic, unpredictable, or chronically stressful environments have nervous systems that are dysregulated.

Daniel Siegel (2010) coined the phrase "window of tolerance" to describe a zone of optimal regulation. This window of tolerance (think of a thermostat that regulates the room temperature) is the place where a person feels comfortable (and safe) and is able to tolerate some highs and some lows. When people are dysregulated and living with chronic stress, they are often outside the window of tolerance. They are either too "hot" (hyperaroused) or too "cold" (hypoaroused). As a teacher, you are responsible for the "temperature" in your classroom. It behooves you to think about the factors that contribute to keeping the temperature in the comfort zone.

A dysregulated nervous system revolves around two states of being: hyperarousal and hypoarousal. In her book *Help for Billy*, Heather Forbes (2012, p. 8) described them as follows:

> **Hyperarousal** is an increase in psychological and physiological tension manifested by a reduction in pain tolerance, increased anxiety, exaggeration of startle responses, insomnia, panic, rage, and an accentuation of personality traits.

> **Hypoarousal** is the decrease in psychological and physiological tension marked by such effects as emotional indifference, flattened affect, irritability, low-grade nervousness, disengagement, depression, and hopelessness.

Students who are experiencing hyperarousal in the classroom might look fidgety; seem unable to stay in their seats; or be disruptive, aggressive, impulsive, or unable to follow directions.

Students who are experiencing hypoarousal in the classroom may look depressed, sleepy, unable to complete work or stay on task, or withdrawn. In fact, they are frequently not even in the class at all. They are absent, tardy, forgetful, and avoidant.

Marianna lumbers into Mr. Blackburn's class late on a Wednesday morning. She hasn't been to school all week and quietly takes her seat in the back of the class. It's frustrating, because she is a really lovely student. She isn't a disciplinary problem, and she is always polite, but she is disengaged and frequently misses school or is often visiting the nurse during class time. She sits for several minutes before Mr. Blackburn notices the top of her desk is still empty. She makes little effort to

(Continued)

(Continued)

get the article and accompanying note-taker that were passed out earlier, and she hasn't made any sign of looking for a pen or notebook. Mr. Blackburn walks over to her, hands her the assignment, and instructs her to join the group next to her. He observes Marianna staring out the window for the rest of the class period and wonders why she doesn't care more about her education. What he doesn't know is that Marianna's parents recently divorced, and she had to move out of the house she grew up in. She'll now be splitting her time between two homes. Marianna is overwhelmed by grief and anxiety; her best coping skill is to sleep. She frequently has stomachaches and is unable to focus. The grief, coupled with feelings of failure (because she knows she isn't doing well in school and her parents will be upset), paralyzes her.

Without understanding the role of regulation, Mr. Blackburn might misinterpret Marianna's behaviors or be quick to label her as a "low" student. In her article "The Low Blow of Labels," Patty McGee (2017) addressed the dangers of labeling students: Describing a child as *low*, "aside from being hurtful, . . . is a nominal fallacy, [which] is the phenomenon where the more the term is used, the less it is understood, the more imprecise the term gets" (p. 1). Better to simply notice the observable behavior and question your interpretations. For example, a hyperaroused kid like Jamie may *look like* a kid who is a class clown, who distracts others, and who is obstinate, annoying, loud, disruptive, or aggressive. Such kids can be the ones whom you find yourself in a power struggle with or the ones who really push your buttons. Conversely, a kid who is hypoaroused, like Marianna, may *look like* a kid who doesn't care, is lazy, doesn't value her education, is a loner, and doesn't try hard enough. You will find strategies for engaging students like Jaime and Marianna as we examine classroom practices in the upcoming sections of this chapter.

Lacking awareness, on both sides of the coin, can create some unhealthy dynamics that break down teacher-student relationships and impede teaching and learning. Students who are functioning in a hyper- or hypoaroused state also lose the ability to function at a relational level. Because students living with chronic stress have not had healthy relationships modeled for them, they are often deficient in those skills too. But just because someone has experienced the impacts of trauma doesn't mean they are forever "stuck" in that way of being. The brain is malleable. Doing something different creates new neural pathways in the brain. If a person "takes a different path," then the old one loses its strength and a new way of being takes shape. The more frequently someone repeats a task or behavior, the larger the "groove" that gets created by the new experience.

People can learn new ways of being and increase their competency when given the right systems and structures that promote safety and growth. Once you start viewing things in terms of self-regulation, the lens shifts. And once the lens shifts, both you and your students have a world of possibilities that were once unimaginable.

Foundation for Effective Practice #2: Strategies for Regulating

People can regulate in two ways: internally and with the help of someone else (externally).

Two Ways to Influence Your Nervous System

Self-regulation (internal) can happen when people practice and deploy skills to help their nervous system relax. Figure 2.2 lists some activities that can become skills to help dial down the intensity of negative thoughts, feelings, and emotions.

Figure 2.2   Things to Do to Help You Calm Down

Deep, slow breathing	Meditation	Mindfulness exercises	Talking to someone	Moving your body
Making lists	Listening to music	Journaling	Coloring	Grounding exercises

These skills are invaluable. And although they seem easy, if you've ever tried to meditate you know that the "simple" act of calming the mind is actually profoundly difficult. A good first step is to take deep, slow breaths. This signals the nervous system to calm down and return to its neutral state of being.

The second way to regulate is to have *external* structures (e.g., people or things in our environment) to help us. As a teacher who commands a classroom full of kids all day long, you have a unique opportunity to help kids regulate. You must be balanced and calm so that your classroom is balanced and calm. Most of the kids in your class are not capable of self-regulation, because they haven't learned the skills. They lack body-awareness and the skills necessary to understand when they are dysregulated and how to fix it. What we know is that with a predictable, safe environment for kids, their nervous systems are able to rest, and then (and only then) can learning take place!

Safety First: The Importance of Physical and Emotional Safety

Safety is paramount to our survival. When we feel safe, we feel calm. When we feel calm, we can learn, and we can take risks to grow. Students who live with chronic stress don't feel safe and often are not safe. Some of them may have experienced trauma and adverse childhood experiences, such as divorce, high expectations for success, abuse, neglect, mental health issues, a family member's addiction, grief, and loss. When safety is compromised and protection is lost, it changes our worldview. People who have experienced a lack of safety don't trust the world around them to be reliable and dependable and kind. They also grow up not knowing how to trust themselves, since trust is built from the outside in. As babies, we trust our primary caregiver to meet our needs for survival. If those needs (emotional or physical) are not met, then we grow up without much opportunity to trust, relax, and grow in a healthy way. When our "fight, flight, or freeze" response is reinforced (due to chronic stress and trauma), using fight or flight as a (solitary) coping skill is also reinforced. That is to say, if we don't develop other skills, fight or flight becomes the only tool in our toolbox.

Although physical safety is a necessity when it comes to cultivating a calm nervous system, emotional safety is an equally important component to learning. When a child lives with chronic stress, failing at a task can *feel* like a threat. For example, students who already struggle to feel calm and confident may find it impossible to ask their teacher a simple clarifying question. The threat of "danger" is too great. As mentioned earlier, one's *perception* of a threat (fear of failure, ridicule, and embarrassment) can be just as powerful as a perceived lack of safety or an actual threat to one's physical self.

You can create safety in the classroom in many ways. The smallest actions and gestures, such as following through with a promise, greeting your students, being transparent, and creating a predictable environment, are great ways to create a sense of both physical and emotional safety. Trust gets built little by little, over time.

Foundation for Effective Practice #3: Don't Take It Personally
Student Behavior: It's Not About You AND It's All About You

> *Nothing others do is because of you. What others say and do is a projection of their own reality, their own dream. When you are immune to the opinions and actions of others, you won't be the victim of needless suffering.*
> —**Miguel Ruiz, *The Four Agreements* (2018)**

All behaviors are adaptive. Everything we do as humans, we do in an effort to get our needs met. That doesn't mean we always do it the "right," healthy, or most effective way, but our intention (whether conscious or unconscious) remains the same. Thinking of other people's behaviors as ways of adapting to a situation helps take the "personal" element out of our interactions. For example, when a student has his head down and seems to be ignoring you, your first instinct may be to attach a negative assumption: *He is so lazy, he just doesn't care.* Instead, you might ask yourself, *What need is he meeting by putting his head down?* Perhaps he is exhausted from something happening at home. Maybe he is feeling overwhelmed because he struggles academically. He may not have eaten a meal today. These are just a few reasons a student might present this way. Now, the kid *could* just be lazy, but the presumption of good intentions and the regulation lens require us to be open to other possibilities.

Being open to looking at student behavior through a strengths-based lens of adaptation can really shift things for you as an educator. Figure 2.3 illustrates a new way of looking at behaviors: through the lens of arousal and regulation.

Figure 2.3   Expanding the Scope of Possibilities for Student Behavior

Student Behavior Observed	Potential Teacher Interpretation and Assumption	Potential Teacher Response	Other Possible Reasons for Observed Behavior: Lens of Arousal	Possible Intervention(s): Things You Can Do	Possible Interventions: Things You Can Say
• The student has his head on his desk.	• *He doesn't care.*	• Ignore student	• Student isn't sleeping • Depression • Lack of self-esteem • Checked out • Shut down	• Nothing—sometimes a student needs space • Acknowledge your observation and offer support	• "I notice you seem really tired. Do you need to get up and get some water?" • "What feels possible for you right now?" • "Would you like to check in with a counselor?"
• The student is late for class.	• *She is irresponsible.* • *She is disrespecting my time.*	• Make sarcastic remark • Harshly remind student of rules	• Demands outside of school • Transportation issues • Lack of parental support • Not sleeping well and therefore not waking up on time	• Initially ignore behavior and then privately and warmly welcome student and help her get on task • Follow up with private conversation after class or in hallway during class	• "I notice you are frequently late to class. I want you to know that your contributions to class matter, and I know how hard it can be for students who come late to get caught up."
• The student makes a disrespectful reply to you.	• *He is just rude.* • *He doesn't like me.* • *He doesn't care.*	• Raise your voice at student • Rashly dismiss student • Publicly demean student	• Triggered by your tone of voice • Overstimulated in classroom • Anxious • Saving face/self-protection from perceived threat	• Ignore it and revisit with student once class is on task, or out in the hallway • Redirect, with warmth • Don't take it personally, and be mindful of the tone and tenor of your response/reaction	• "Hey, I notice you snapped at me—what do you think we need to do to change the way we interact?" • "I am open to doing something different, and I hope you are too."

(Continued)

(Continued)

Student Behavior Observed	Potential Teacher Interpretation and Assumption	Potential Teacher Response	Other Possible Reasons for Observed Behavior: Lens of Arousal	Possible Intervention(s): Things You Can Do	Possible Interventions: Things You Can Say
• The student is disrupting other students.	• *She doesn't listen.* • *She doesn't care.* • *She's disrespectful.* • *She's seeking attention or on a power trip.*	• Harshly confront student, make cutting remark	• Hyperarousal • Overstimulation • Covering up lack of confidence in content area/knowledge	• Help the student chunk assignment into smaller, doable bits • Check in frequently, with praise for specific effort/work	• "Hey, I notice you are not focused right now. Do you need to get a drink of water or perhaps sit somewhere less stimulating to do your work?" • "Do you need to step out for a minute to regroup?"
• The student is not participating in small-group work.	• *He is apathetic, waiting for others to do the work.*	• Nag or lecture student about participating, demean student	• Social or emotional issue that prompts student to withdraw out of fear, being overwhelmed, exhaustion, or self-preservation	• Use empathy and lean in to let student know you are aware that she/he is not participating • Express concern about why student is not participating	• Consider a private conversation so as not to shame student in front of his/her peers • "How can I support you in participating?" • "May I help clarify the task?" • "What steps might you take toward full participation?"

If you are willing to assume your students have positive intentions, to not take things too personally, and to be curious and empathetic, your relationships with students and your classroom culture will shift out of power/control and into cooperation and connection. Imagine how much more effective and enjoyable your job will be without so much of your energy wasted on power struggles. This strategy provides a win-win for the relationship and, subsequently, for teaching and learning.

Mindset matters. There is a mindset that is required to be successful in this model that focuses on creating a safe environment and healthy relationships in the classroom. It's not just a mindset; it's the creation of a new way of being. Utilizing specific practices (mindfulness, meditation, breathing, open-mindedness) in order to be calm and grounded will help you deal with disruptions as they show up. Choosing to increase your awareness of your own mindset, while being more intentional in your reactions, will help you notice when things are subtly shifting from calm toward chaos. Figure 2.4 highlights how mindset affects the continuum of calm.

Figure 2.4 The Continuum of Calm

More of this . . .	Less of that . . .
Calm	Chaos
Confident (*I am an adult*, "I got this.")	*I don't got this, and they'll know it.*
Stepping into a role of "Observer"—*It's not personal to me.*	*They are doing this to me.*
Taking a moment to pause and regroup (both yourself and the classroom)	Steamrolling forward when things aren't working (for you or for them)
Transparency	Secrets/surprises
Naming behaviors	Getting personal
Allow students to save face	Needing to save face yourself
Provide students an opportunity to opt out, calm down, and rejoin	Forcing them to opt in when they are dysregulated
Patience	Impatience/irritability
Humor	Sarcasm
Acceptance	Judgment
Praise	Criticism
Cooperation	Power and control
Asking for help	Working in isolation
Taking care of yourself, using healthy coping skills to manage life stress	Ignoring yourself and using unhealthy coping skills to manage life stress

What Works in the Classroom: Cultivating Self-Regulation

Every organism needs an environment (a biome) in order to thrive—a place that is safe, predictable, reliable, and, at times, even when hostile, offers some modicum of protection. Biological studies point to all living organisms' continual search to reach *homeostasis*—a relatively stable state of equilibrium. When faced with change, threat, or scarcity, the organism naturally attempts to stabilize itself. It is a matter of survival. In a parallel aspect, classrooms are environments where those who live within them need assurance that elements for survival exist and that the "temperature" is just right. Students need a supportive environment or they will seek to move on.

Certainly, the educational environment may not be as extreme in nature as reptilian habitats, per se; for many students, it may be the most stable environment they encounter. The reliability of particular systems and structures is paramount to whether students experience safety and dependability of resources. Take a moment to reflect, both now and throughout the day: *Is my classroom environment offering students emotional safety, calm, and opportunities to thrive? How am I feeling right now?* Students' experiences in classrooms like yours will determine whether they stay with it—that is, show up in both body and mind—or seek another alternative, such as absence, avoidance, or inattention.

Since the classroom biome is vital to student growth and progress, there are three systems and structures particularly worthy of close examination: consistency, clear expectations, and movement.

Be Consistently Consistent

Rituals and routines are elements of an effective lesson design that creates regulating habits for both students and teachers. Teachers should plan and incorporate a consistent set of elements that begin the moment students enter the room and last through the end of the lesson when students are walking out. Grant Wiggins and Jay McTighe (2008) said of lesson design: "To use an analogy with storytelling, a story needs a plot, characters, and setting. But how should those elements be fashioned into the most engaging and effective whole? There are many possible beginnings, middles, and ends" (p. 198). Every good lesson, like a good story, needs a beginning, a middle, and an end.

Victor is an average 11th-grader who, most days, has six class periods, with block periods twice a week. For him, experiencing consistency in how a typical lesson is constructed helps him focus less on how the class is going to roll out and more on the "cognitive load" (Duhigg, 2014)—the thinking and meaning-making within the content. Such consistency is balanced with interesting and varied learning activities that keep students engaged. When class begins the same way, runs through a relatively consistent routine, and then ends in a familiar way, Victor is focusing on what he is learning, not on what is taking place procedurally. He is used to how his classes operate; he can anticipate the order of events. If each of Victor's teachers utilizes the same or similar routines, then he is not dedicating precious teenage energy to "code switching" between teachers; rather, his primary concern is the difference in content. Not only is Victor focusing on what will help him gain competency, but also he is feeling calm and confident in what his day looks like. This is regulating.

Schools are increasingly stressful places to be. There are potential and real uncertainties to our days that sometimes keep us up at night. Routines keep us moving forward in a consistent manner in the face of stressors such as absences, sickness, fatigue, worry, conflict, and catastrophe.

Set Clear Expectations in the Classroom: For Them and You

For teachers to set clear expectations in the classroom environment, and for students to follow through, there needs to be a high level of clarity regarding expectations related to process, task, time, space, and place.

Clarity of Process

For most course offerings, teachers have descriptions in place that identify the expected outcomes of the class; the required text and learning materials; grading scales; and a general description of assignments. Typically, teachers have the academic piece covered. However, are there expectations outlined in your classroom policies for dealing with behavior, specifically with a student who is dysregulated? What is your plan for interacting with a student who breaks down in tears, drops an F-bomb, or is openly defiant? Along those same lines, what is the plan for when interactions become chaotic, escalated, or simply "out of control"?

If you've been in a school for even a short time, you can attest to the reality that things go awry. As teachers, we plan for one thing, and another happens—in other words, the actual outcome does not match the intended outcome. For this reason, you have to plan for the reality of life in your classroom, while aiming to set high expectations that frame a high-functioning learning environment. In her book *Mindset*, Carol Dweck (2008) maintained that "Great teachers set high standards for all their students, not just the ones who are already achieving. . . . Yet [they also] establish . . . an atmosphere of genuine affection and concern" (p. 196).

"Share the secret" with students. Having a transparent plan that supports high expectations, emanates care, and provides choice is an effective practice. It need not be complicated or require a counseling degree. Share the plan in a syllabus, post it publicly, and reiterate it throughout the school year. As an example, Figure 2.5 shows how Ms. Cummings sets out five simple and straightforward expectations for student and teacher behavior.

Figure 2.5   Classroom Expectations in Ms. Cummings's Classroom

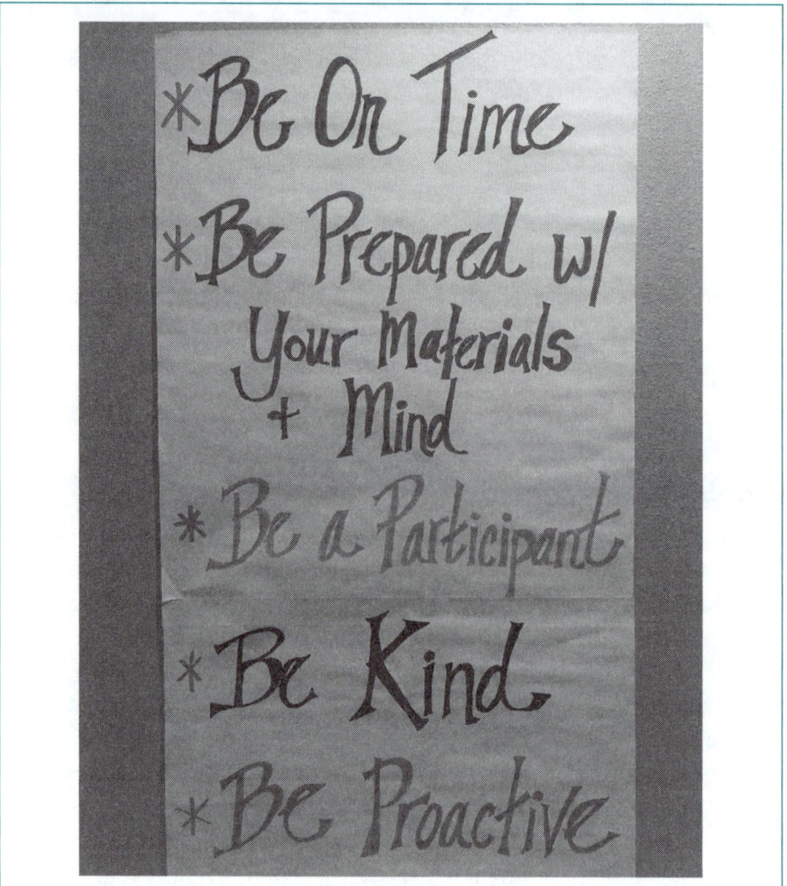

Next, she writes out steps that will help a student regulate should these expectations not be met for whatever reason. Notice the suggestions that she includes in her syllabus.

Life is not perfect, and, as people, we are not either. Being proactive means taking steps to take care of yourself. Please know that I care and will follow up on your choices: If tardy . . . settle in and join in. If confused . . . ask for help. If angry . . . take a moment to breathe, and/or let me know that you need to get a drink. If you can't manage . . . let me know that you need to check in with the counselor immediately. Our school is full of adults who want to help you help yourself.

In other words, she intentionally addresses emotional regulation, with the same clarity as she would other elements that constitute a high-functioning class. Stating, in advance, clear expectations for classroom life in the face of potential dysregulation will help a chaotic situation return to a calm one.

Clarity of Task

For students to be successful, they need to understand what that involves. Make no assumptions that students just "get it." In fact, teachers frequently hear from students, "Now what are we supposed to do?" after having been provided verbal directions. Or "Will we get a grade for this?" "How many pages does it need to be?" "Should we use complete sentences?" Rubrics, exemplars, criteria for success, and checklists provide students a clear understanding of what is being asked of them. Certainly, the more complex the task, the more specificity you need. That said, in any particular lesson, students also need to be aware of what they are supposed to produce—the guidelines not only for completion, but also for quality. As John Hattie (2012) advocated in *Visible Learning for Teachers and Students*, teachers "must not make the mistake of making success criteria relate merely to completing the activity or a lesson being engaging; instead, the major role is to get students engaged in and enjoying the challenge of learning" (p. 570). Student work products might consist of a well-written conclusion, a rich text-based discussion, a correctly answered problem, a detailed drawing, an insightful question, or a thoughtful solution. In each case, the teacher should communicate what earning full points would look like.

It is critical to provide clarity about student behavior within the given task, as well. Mr. Douglas, a science teacher, consistently names for students their responsibilities in individual, small-group, and whole-class contexts. He indicates to them what task they are to attend to and the work product they are to produce—for example, "Read and annotate the article from *Scientific American*, then be prepared to discuss." During labs, he is clear that students are to work as a team, conducting the experiment, recording the data, and answering the questions individually in their notebooks. He also is explicit about sharing the workload and that there should be no "free riders." When asked for the hundredth time, he calmly replies, "Yes, you each will record the data in your lab notebooks." While they record the data, he is an instructional rover—he monitors groups to ensure that each student is participating, as well as provides targeted instruction. He continues to "share the secret" about what constitutes success.

Clarity of Time

Time may be the most valuable commodity in the world of education. Time creates a container for great things to take place. It's used most effectively when both teachers and students are aware of how it's being used—in other words, when:

- there is transparency;

- the teacher monitors time throughout the lesson to help students be conscious of time;

- time frames are provided; and

- reminders of time remaining are offered.

For example: "You will have 30 minutes to review the film clip and to discuss the five questions. Record responses in complete sentences. The film is about 11 minutes; that leaves about 19 minutes for the questions. I will check in with you when 15 minutes remain, then again at 5 minutes. Identify someone who will help monitor time in your group." The point is not to create anxiety, but rather to create awareness and a sense of control of how time is spent. Knowledge of time and its usage drives effective decision-making.

Clarity of Space and Place

Classrooms are sacred spaces. What happens on any given day can be magical, average, or challenging—mirroring other aspects of life. Teachers can provide an increased sense of security and balance in the way they manage their classroom space. Think about how features of spaces you know have an effect on your perception. If a space is messy, littered, or dark, you most likely infer that things are unsettled or unattended. This may leave the impression that something is awry. If a space is orderly, clean, and well-lit, it seems like someone is paying attention and alert. Things seem like they are under control.

Desk structures send messages about power dynamics and voice. Figure 2.6 shows two classrooms: collaborative versus one-directional. If learning is collaborative, student desks reflect this value by being in various groupings. The implication is that each voice has a place at the table. Conversely, if all desks face one direction, students may infer that the voice up front is the one that matters most. That person has the power. Feeling powerless signals the mind to be on alert—the opposite of calm.

Figure 2.6   Classroom Configurations to Support Collaborative vs. One-Directional Learning

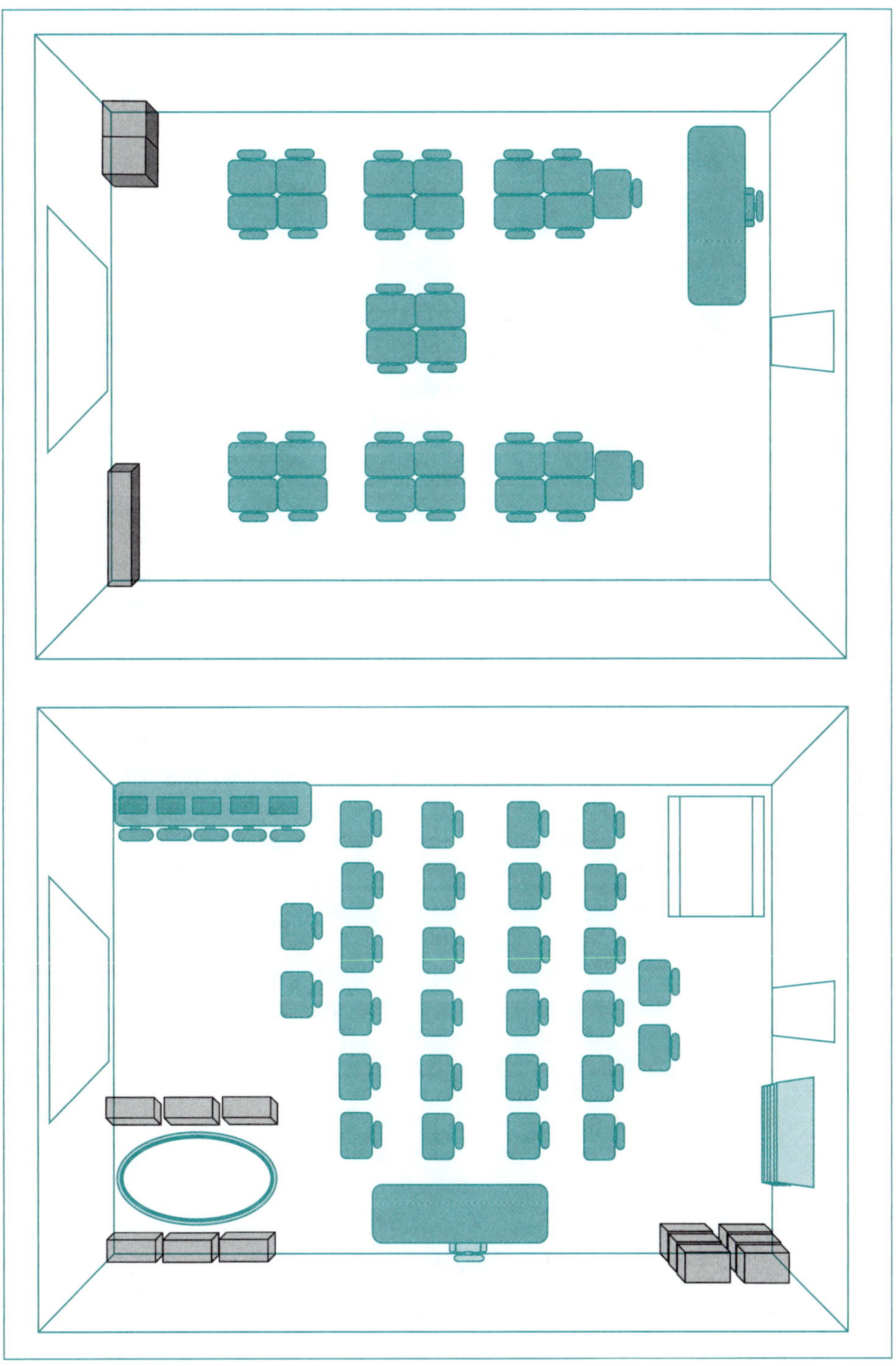

Source: Reprinted with permission from *The Movement and Technology Balance: Classroom Strategies for Student Success* (2019). Copyright © 2020 by Traci Lengel and Jenna Evans.

Finally, it is worth considering a seating chart, especially if everyone is new to the classroom. It provides students their own space, yet allows for flexibility when modifications are needed, such as for student learning and interpersonal needs. At the beginning of a term, when you use a seating chart it gives students a sense of space and place, and it gives you a means of learning their names as quickly as possible. Over time, most teachers rearrange the seating chart, while others let it go entirely. After getting to know students and the class culture, you can make informed decisions regarding seating. Last—like most of the adults in the school, who sit in the same location during faculty meetings or conferences, park in the same parking place, and eat at the same lunch spot—students need a place of their own. This creature comfort is something that we can all relate to.

Let's see how it might look or what it might sound like to coordinate task, time, space, and place. Figure 2.7 provides some suggestions for doing so transparently throughout a lesson. Note how all three areas tend to interconnect.

Keep 'Em Moving

Asking a student to sit quietly and focus while unsettled, or for an extended period of time, contradicts what we know in regulating the brain. Think of the last time you had to sit through an all-day faculty meeting. Did you want to crawl out of your skin? Did you have trouble staying awake and on task? Perhaps you dreamed of going to lunch and then for a walk. Like adults, students need to move their bodies throughout the class period. As Daniel Siegel (2011) stated, "research shows that when we change our physical state—through movement or relaxation, for example—we change our emotional state" (p. 58).

How do you incorporate movement into your lesson designs? How can you accommodate more movement in order to support student regulation? It may be necessary, and would probably be wise, to consult a peer, a school counselor, or an administrator in an effort to design a plan that is workable for when a student needs to step out of class for a few moments. It would be regrettable to offer students options that might create more stress, like leaving to get a sip of water only to receive an infraction for being in the hall.

Figure 2.7   Using Transparency in Time, Task, and Space/Place

	Beginning	Middle	End
Task and Time	"Good morning. Please take a look at the Do Now. Recall what you know about the 10 Principles of the UN Global Compact. Next, highlight three that your group discussed yesterday. In writing, share your thinking about why your group selected each. Be prepared to share." "You have 5 to 7 minutes to activate your mind. Now, go!" [Student comes in tardy. Teacher says, "Welcome, Marty. You will have to work more quickly to complete the Do Now. You have about 3 minutes. Please get started. Thank you."]	"You have will have roughly 12 minutes to collaborate with your group. Be sure to monitor the time. Take a look at the clock. Talk with one another about what time it will be when you need to be ready to share. Write it down somewhere in your notes, if you need to." "Take a look at the clock. Talk with your group about how much time remains. Prioritize what your group needs to do within that time frame." "May I have your attention in one minute, please?" "May I have your attention, please. Five. Four. Three. Two. One. Thank you."	"We have 4 minutes remaining in the class period. Please take out your note-taker and answer the exit ticket that is on the board. When you are finished, please share your thinking with your partner." "Here's my 10-second recap as your teacher. Thank you for using your time so effectively today. I observed each group making an effort to listen to one another, offer thoughtful insights, and ensure that each member had time to share his or her thoughts. Well done."
Space and Place	Students have assigned seats. After the first part of the year or new semester, there is opportunity for students to select their seats. The teacher can always make adjustments as needed.	"You and your group will need to face one another, so turn your desks in order to see eyeball to eyeball with them. Smile; aren't they fabulous? If you need a little more room to spread out with your materials, please let me know. It's important that you are comfortable and have space to do your work."	"As you leave today, please make sure your space is free of trash. Please push in your chair. Thank you. This is a sacred space, so let's keep it tidy. Enjoy the rest of your day."

Taking Self-Regulation School-Wide

Every school has policies in place to address dysregulated students. Most schools primarily respond to disruptive student behaviors with punitive measures like detention, expulsion, and suspension. When self-regulation becomes a proactive rather than reactive approach to working with students, leadership has the opportunity to modify several areas of the school's operations related to space, discipline, and environment.

Safe Spaces

Administration may identify spaces (e.g., a designated "quiet room," student commons, cafeteria, courtyard, or counseling office) for students to go when they need a moment to reset. Leaders encourage teachers to provide options for students when allowing them to leave the classroom that are safe and regulating in nature. We know of several schools that offer students options to check in at the library for this purpose. It's important that these spaces be known by the entire school community and be as nearby classrooms as possible.

Culture of Discipline

The discussion around student behavior leads to the important topic of discipline. To many, this may be the least savory aspect of school leadership. It is where students are perceived to be at their worst (i.e., most dysregulated) selves—and, in some cases, where the adults are, as well. Addressing student behavior is more an aspect of school culture than it is about policies. It presents the leadership team the opportunity to explore the relationship between beliefs about student behavior and the policies that inform them: "What are we trying to achieve with our approach to discipline? Do our policies help support student regulation? Do they create a safe and well-resourced environment for students to thrive? Lastly, what skill set does our administrative team need to build in order to lead in this effort?"

Leadership in this highly charged and critical area is about anticipating stressful situations whereby people fail to behave as required (i.e., according to the rules) and about using systems and structures to restore balance. School disciplinary policies have the opportunity to provide regulation and calm, particularly when leadership is clear that these are school priorities. We will look more in depth at conflict resolution and school discipline in Chapter 6.

Environmental Preservation

School leaders can preserve the hard work of classroom teachers in maintaining a calm environment by mitigating interruptions. They can help curb the use of the intercom for communication that can be handled by other means. Additionally, policies that reduce the incidence of other people entering the classroom and demanding instructional time can help mitigate distractions. It's difficult to recover from disruptions. Leadership needs to support teachers and their students in maintaining both routine and focus.

Reflections

Teaching is a big job; it's intense, in fact. Spending your days with adolescents is not for the weak or faint of heart. You owe it to yourself and to your students to stay calm, slow down, and rely on best practices to keep the classroom running smoothly.

Take a moment to think about the following questions, then jot down your responses.

1. Under what circumstances in my classroom do I feel the most out of control?

2. What keeps me balanced?

3. What concerns me about this topic?

4. I wonder about . . .

5. What feels possible about all of this?

Toolkit for Tomorrow

In an effort to cultivate self-regulation, tomorrow I can:

- ❑ understand how hyperarousal and hypoarousal might look in my classroom.
- ❑ be aware of how I might react to students who are dysregulated.
- ❑ check my mindset.
- ❑ identify a plan for regulating myself in the face of student dysregulation.
- ❑ identify a plan for how class time is going to be used.
- ❑ design a plan for how class space will be used.
- ❑ share with students clear expectations for learning tasks.
- ❑ share with students clear expectations for peer-to-peer interactions.
- ❑ use healthy boundaries.
- ❑ lead with compassion . . . for myself and for others.

In the End, Be Loving

In order to stay regulated, you must stay in your adult self, presume good intentions, and rise above the fray. Don't take things too personally. Students like Jamie and Marianna are doing the best they can, and so are you. Your challenge is to stay calm, step back, and see beyond the behavior to the person underneath. At the end of the day, your role as a loving and stable presence will help your classroom be a loving, calm place to learn and grow.

Self-Care

Check Yourself Before You Wreck Yourself

Sometimes the most important thing in a whole day
is the rest we take between two breaths.

—Etty Hillesum

On a Monday morning in late November, Ms. Patel pulls into the full school parking lot. Cold and windblown, she struggles to hold onto her coffee mug, lunch bag, purse, and tote bag—overflowing with student work. Hurriedly, she rushes into the school building with less than five minutes to spare before the first-period bell rings. Reeling from the chaos of a Thanksgiving weekend with family, she is regretting the decision to arrive back home late last night, instead of giving herself some time back at her apartment. The planning and grading session on the two-hour flight didn't exactly accomplish all that she had hoped, so she won't be handing back the papers she had promised to the kids today.

She feels irritable, exhausted, and rushed as she blows past some students and enters her classroom. Lights . . . on. Computer . . . on. The students stroll in with their sleepy eyes and morning groans. Ms. Patel knows she must press on with the new history project, as finals are just around the corner, even though she has yet to return the last two weeks of graded work. The bell rings as she wearily asks students to take their seats. With a giant swig of coffee, she wonders how many days until winter break . . . as another day begins.

Self-Care: Why Is It Important?

Teaching is a vocation that involves long hours, low pay, classrooms stuffed with kids, grading, lunch duty, coaching, tutoring, planning, chaperoning dances, attending sports events, and state-mandated testing. What kind of people are inspired to take a job like this? People like you—kind, passionate, intellectual, caring, loving, selfless, idealists who *want to make a difference in this world*. For many, teaching is a calling. Some are drawn to this work in an effort to give back what they themselves received. Others are in it to ensure that students get what they themselves did not. Many were inspired by great teachers who changed the course of their lives. The single greatest impact on student learning and formation is the one made by high-quality, passionate teachers (Hattie, 2012). This noble work comes at a cost, which can include burnout and poor physical, financial, and emotional health. If you don't attend to and care for yourself, you won't last in this profession.

Student Experience

Teacher stress impacts students' stress. Because students with chronic stress and trauma need their teachers to be clear, present, and loving, they are easily derailed if the teacher is unable to effectively attend to their needs or the needs of the class. In Chapter 2, we highlighted the importance of the teacher being a regulator of the class. If the teacher is dysregulated by symptoms of burnout or vicarious trauma, the students and learning will suffer. In 2016, University of British Columbia researchers tracked the levels of stress hormones of more than 400 elementary students in different classes. They found that teachers who reported higher levels of burnout had students with higher levels of the stress hormone cortisol each morning, suggesting that classroom tensions are "contagious" (Sparks, 2017). Teachers need to make their own health a priority, so that they can co-regulate and be effective in their life's work.

Adult Experience

Overcrowded classrooms, underfunded schools, long hours, and students who experience increased mental health issues related to chronic stress and trauma often leave teachers feeling more like first responders than educators. As an educator–first responder, you are tasked with having to make split-second decisions on the front lines, often alone. This work takes a heavy toll. And because you are a selfless, loving, caring individual who was drawn to this work to make an impact on students' lives, it is most likely that you put *yourself* at the bottom of the list of things to take care of. You may find yourself thinking things like *I don't know how much longer I can do this*, or *Why is this so hard for me, when it seems like others have it easy? When is the next school break?* You are not alone. Teachers often find themselves overwhelmed and stressed out, which can lead to physical, psychological, and spiritual illness.

The first step in preventing burnout is to increase your awareness of its symptoms, causes, and impact. The next step is to identify what strategies are most helpful for you to attend to your needs. Figure 3.1 provides some reflection questions for your consideration in an effort to (re)ignite your passion for the work. There is no bigger heart than the heart of an educator.

Figure 3.1 What Your Heart Knows . . .

Why did you choose to be an educator?

____

____

____

What qualities do you possess that make you a good educator?

____

____

____

What do you love most about this work?

____

____

____

Foundation for Effective Practice #1: Avoiding Burnout

Teacher burnout rates are higher than ever. More than 41% of teachers leave the profession within the first five years (Ingersoll, Merrill, & Stuckey, 2014); in total, approximately half a million, or 15% of teachers, leave the profession every year (Haynes, 2014). These statistics don't acknowledge the vast number of teachers who stay in the field while wrestling with symptoms of burnout. What many fail to realize is that burnout is actually work-induced depression. According to research published in the _Journal of Clinical Psychology_, there is a significant overlap between burnout and depression. More specifically, educators experiencing burnout simultaneously exhibit depressive symptoms, including, but not limited to, loss of interest or pleasure in activities, mood swings, and fatigue (Diaz, 2018).

Burnout happens slowly and over time. It commonly occurs among people whose identity is strongly connected with their work, at those times when the work has become discouraging, hopeless, disappointing, or less meaningful. It isn't that teachers can't handle the job, so much as they feel they aren't getting the support they need to handle the stressors associated with teaching. We all know that teachers are underpaid, are under-resourced, and are under high expectations to produce results. But in today's schools, the impact of chronic stress on both teacher and student make it extra challenging for teachers to stay healthy, balanced, prepared, and passionate.

The good news about burnout is that, if you recognize the symptoms early enough, you may only need to make minor adjustments. Perhaps spending a few days away, updating your self-care plan, bolstering your support systems, reading a good book, or having dinner with a friend will help turn things around. Staying mindful of your burnout warning signs (see Figure 3.3) will help you recognize the symptoms earlier and enable you to attend to your needs.

No teacher ever wants someone to think that they don't care about kids or aren't willing to put in the hard work to make a difference in a student's life. Therefore teachers often sacrifice themselves, internalize things they have no control over, try harder, do more, feel discouraged, and blame others, and it's easy to spiral into apathy, anger, or despair. Without self-care practices, this cycle usually ends up in burnout at best or breakdown at worst. Figure 3.2 represents this cycle of burnout that you may recognize having experienced at some point in your career. Notice if this feels familiar or you see yourself anywhere on this diagram.

This cycle comes with associated symptoms that manifest when your needs are not met and adjustments are not made. Figure 3.3 lists some of the symptoms of burnout. Do you recognize any of them?

Figure 3.2   The Cycle of Burnout

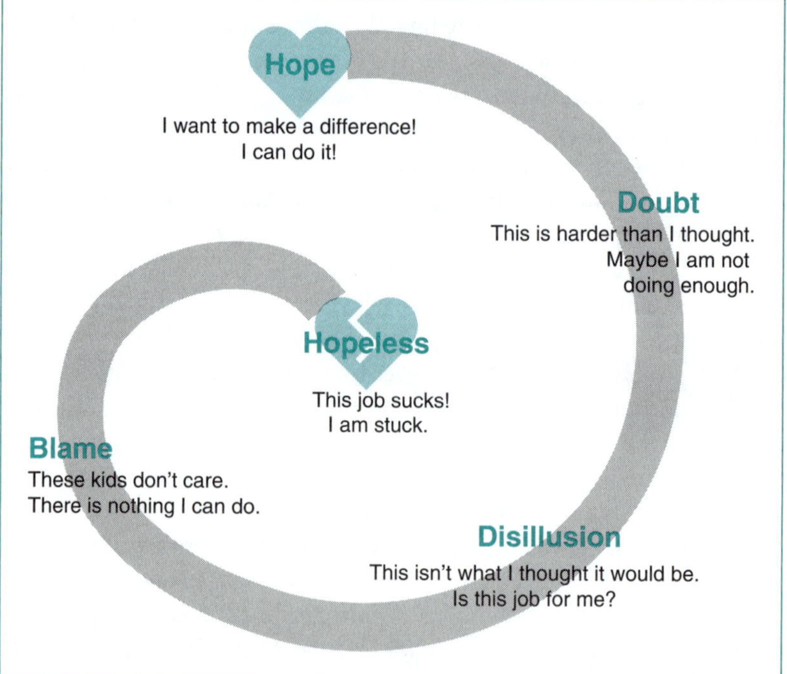

Source: Figure layout by Bill Grimmer.

Figure 3.3 Simple Symptoms of the Sizzle

Lack of patience	Being late for work
Irritability	Looking for other jobs
Poor planning	Apathy
Lack of motivation	Blaming others
Missing work	Complaining
Not attending to daily tasks	Checking out

What are some of your warning signs that you are starting to sizzle?

1. ____

____

2. ____

____

3. ____

____

4. ____

____

Foundation for Effective Practice #2: Recognizing Vicarious Trauma

There is a condition that is more significant than burnout, commonly known in other helping professions—such as ER physicians, police, firefighters, therapists, and other first responders—as *vicarious trauma*. The American Counseling Association (ACA, 2011) defines "vicarious trauma" as a state of tension and preoccupation with the stories/trauma experiences described by clients (students). And although you are a teacher or a coach and not a therapist or a police officer, you are still at risk of being impacted by the stories of the students with whom you work. Vicarious trauma happens when you can no longer tolerate hearing about or witnessing someone's trauma. It is often accompanied by a sense of helplessness and hopelessness.

Ms. Fisher goes to the counselor's office in tears, holding a piece of paper crumpled in her hand. It's a short story that a student had written that was both touching and disturbing. She sits there, first apologizing for her tears and then saying: "I can't stop thinking about this student. Our kids have such hard lives—I can't imagine the struggles they go through. How do they show up at school each day

(Continued)

(Continued)

while this kind of thing is going on at home?" As she waves the paper toward the counselor's face, she bends her head and sobs into her hands. The counselor listens as she continues: "What is the point? I mean, how are things ever going to get better in the world? I don't know why I am even teaching; I am so tired. What is the point? Nothing we do matters."

Now, those of us who work with kids know that some of them share stories of hardship and heartache. And it isn't the fact that Ms. Fisher was upset by the story that is concerning. It is her deep hopelessness, her ruminating about the student, her exhaustion, and the intensity of her emotion that illustrate her vicarious trauma. After years of reading student work and absorbing the feelings that came up for her, without attending to her own self-care needs, Ms. Fisher is now herself experiencing symptoms of trauma that she did not experience firsthand (vicarious).

Listed in Figure 3.4 are some of the ways that the ACA defines the signs and symptoms of vicarious trauma.

Figure 3.4   Symptoms of Vicarious Trauma

• Tardiness	• Avoiding being alone
• Free-floating anger/irritability	• Hopelessness
• Worried about not doing enough	• Dropping out of community affairs
• Absenteeism	• Rejecting physical/emotional closeness
• Irresponsibility	• Staff conflict
• Overwork	• Detachment
• Irritability	• Blaming others
• Exhaustion	• Conflict
• Talking to oneself (a critical symptom)	• Poor relationships
• Lack of collaboration	• Poor communication
• Withdrawal and isolation from colleagues	• Impatience
• Negative perception	• Avoiding work that has to do with trauma
• Questioning one's own beliefs/worldview/ spirituality	• Difficulty in having rewarding relationships

Source: Fact Sheet #9: Vicarious Trauma, (2011). American Counseling Association. www.counseling.org

If you recognize yourself in this symptom list and suspect you may be experiencing vicarious trauma, please consider meeting with a mental health professional to get some support for yourself. This phenomenon is more common than you think, and there is nothing *deficient in you* because you are struggling in this work. In fact, it is because you are so caring that you are vulnerable to vicarious trauma. You owe it to yourself and your students to get support if you need it.

Foundation for Effective Practice #3: Navigating Mixed Messages and Cultural Norms

Why is it that society's narrative about helping professionals like first responders and teachers is that they are willing to accept "payment" not in dollars but in the intrinsic "rewards" associated with doing good work and making a difference? Being underpaid isn't just a narrative; it's a cultural norm. Take salaries, for example; teachers are paid 21.4% less than similarly educated and experienced professionals, according to a recent Economic Policy Institute (EPI) report, which found that the "teacher pay gap" recently reached a record high (EPI, 2018). No wonder it is hard for teachers to maintain good financial health with today's cost of living. Take a minute to reflect on the different kinds of investments and sacrifices you have made for this career. They are important and worth protecting. This is another reason why self-care matters.

Figure 3.5 provides some questions for your reflection on your path to being an educator.

Figure 3.5   Reflections on the Journey to Becoming an Educator

Describe your path to this career.

____

____

How much time and money have you invested in your education?

____

____

What sacrifices, both personal and professional, have you made for your career?

____

____

Being underpaid is just one aspect of the cultural norm that sends the message that in order to be a "good teacher" (read: good person), you must make sacrifices—you have to work long hours, have poor financial health, say "yes" to everything, do more, and be selfless. Are these messages explicit? No, but the culture and perception of education send these types of messages nonetheless. This view supports a sort of martyr mindset that makes it difficult for teachers to identify and ask for what they need. Figure 3.6 shows what can happen when the very character traits that drew you to this profession warp into poor professional and personal health.

Figure 3.6   Too Much of a Good Thing: When Good Intentions Go Wrong

Best Intentions	Worst Outcomes
Desire to help	Enabling others
Doing more because needs are great	Disillusionment and resentment
Wanting to connect with students	Having your emotional needs met by students instead of healthy adults
Wanting to be a part of something bigger	Becoming enmeshed and losing your individual identity
Caring for others	Neglecting your own needs
Wanting to make a difference	Pushing your agenda on others

What Works in the Classroom: Translating Self-Care Into Teaching and Learning Practices

If you are feeling hopeless, don't despair. It is possible to create work-life balance and maintain vitality, good health, and joy in this profession. Taking care of yourself on a personal level is the predicate for taking care of yourself on a professional level. In teaching, this principle nudges us to examine several core areas of practice in order to develop a sustainable and generative career. The following section is filled with strategies to help you mitigate chronic stress, reduce burnout and vicarious trauma, and increase self-care. The foundational principles are as follows:

- Less is more—the art of sifting, sorting, and letting go

- Patterns—the art of recognizing ruts, drains, and seasons that impact your work

- Sustainability—the art of creating personal and professional planning habits

Less Is More

Time. Because you're a salaried employee, your day does not begin and end when the bell rings. You have hours of grading, planning, supply-gathering, parent conferences, worry, stress, and strain that last long after the final bell of the day. In many school cultures, whether implicitly or explicitly stated, there are expectations for teachers to attend dances, games, staff parties, fundraisers, field trips, plays, and so much more. One of the strongest tensions that exists in the realm of self-care is *wanting to participate* in or support students with extracurricular programming and *needing time away from school.* Figure 3.7 is meant to help you identify how your time is spent, so that you may make conscious choices about how to spend your time in future.

Figure 3.7   Where Does All the Time Go?

Take an assessment of how much time you are spending at your job:

In an average week, how many hours do you spend teaching/working?________________

In an average week, how many hours do you spend outside of school on planning?________ On grading?________

In an average week, how many hours do you spend supervising or participating in extracurricular school-related activities? ____________________________________

Write those numbers below, and add them up:

___ hours spent teaching/working
___ hours spent planning
___ hours spent grading
___ hours of extracurricular school-related activities

56 hours of sleep (8 hours a night), if you are *lucky*

___ **Total number of hours, including sleep**

Take the total and subtract it from 168 hours (the number of hours in a week) 168 – _____ = _____

That is the number of hours you have left in an average week for family, friends, laundry, shopping, cooking, cleaning, resting, and Netflix.

Given that time is one of the greatest commodities we have, it is helpful to consider ways to protect it. Here are some strategies you might consider:

- Use a color-coded calendar to document actual time spent for a month. Notice patterns, and create changes as needed.

- List ways you can manage your time more effectively.

- Identify what is most important in your job and what is secondary. Let the most important thing *be* the most important thing.

- Say "no" to things that pull you out of balance. Set limits.

Designing curriculum by focusing on what matters most. Even the most effective teachers can't teach everything. There are not enough days in the school year and minutes during the week to cover all that is *required* in most curriculum maps, scope and sequences, and unit plans. Something has to go. Operating under the premise that preserving and sustaining resources, namely time and effort, forces educators to name what matters most. For years, we have encouraged teachers to be brave and to remove the clutter in order to name what is most meaningful. Education gurus like Grant Wiggins and Jay McTighe in *Understanding by Design* (2008) pushed educators to identify *essential understandings* and clearly *defined performance tasks* more than a decade ago. Expeditionary Learning Education, for example, offers an entire school design founded on the "less is more" principle, one that crafts learning endeavors that focus both students and teachers on fewer topics and skills while aiming for excellence in student character and high-quality student work. These curricular and systemic efforts live out the belief that some things are more important than others to learn; therefore, they must be prioritized. This pursuit requires bravery on behalf of teachers and leaders if learning is to be about uncovering and discovering, not just covering content (Wiggins & McTighe, 2008).

Upon reflection, caring for ourselves and for our students demands that we, as educators, curate teaching and learning experiences. This can be an uncomfortable experience, especially if the expectation is that we cover everything. Teachers have to be brave in advocating for doing fewer things better in order to sustain effective practice. Taking action requires asking the following questions: "With whom do I consult—a curriculum director, department head, fellow teacher, or mentor—in order to help me determine what matters most?" "If there is not a resource in my building, where might I turn for guidance?" You are never alone, so seek out support; you'll find someone. Additionally, with accessibility to online teacher groups, professional organizations, and blogs, it's feasible to reach out to the larger teaching community for ideas and support. Figure 3.8 provides elements to consider in practicing *less is more* in curriculum design in order to focus on what matters most within limited instructional time.

Figure 3.8   Elements of "Less Is More" in Curriculum Design

Less	More
Time learning many topics	Time investigating fewer topics
Time covering topics	Time dedicated to uncovering and discovering topics
Emphasis on surface-level facts	Emphasis on deeper meaning
Recitation	Creation
Quizzes, tests	Formative assessment, summative performance tasks
Units of study	Exploration of topics

Workflow that flows. Time is both a teacher's greatest asset and a teacher's biggest nemesis. Scarcity of time forces you to identify what matters most in curriculum, instruction, and assessment. When you're considering what matters most in regard to using this precious commodity, Figure 3.9 outlines a process to help you make decisions while implementing the "less is more" principle. Ask yourself, *What matters most as I step through the planning process?*

Teachers can't possibly give a grade to every piece of classwork or homework. Sustainable practices dictate that some assignments will matter more than others as a measure of what students know. Most student work products provide insight into students' progress toward desired learning intentions, although not each one will be given a grade. In fact, most won't. The point of student work is to provide proof of student learning (or not learning) along the way, whereby students are aware of their progress throughout

Figure 3.9 Teacher Workflow: What Matters Most?

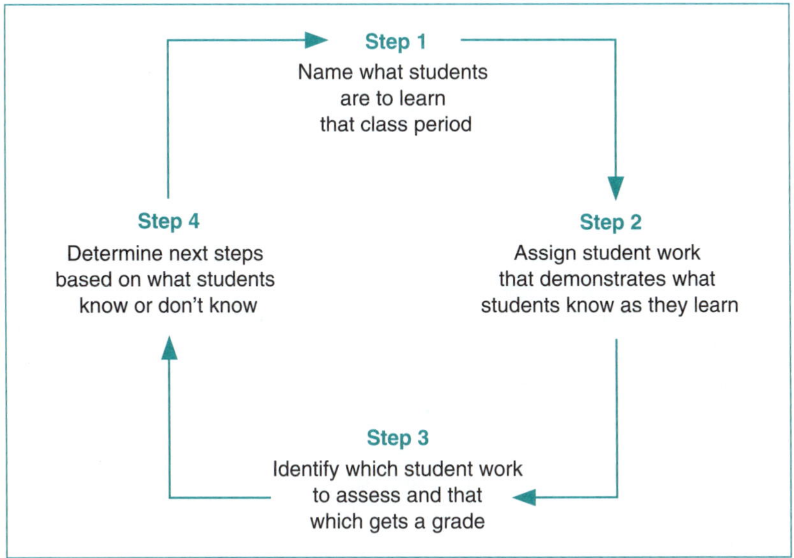

Source: Figure layout by Bill Grimmer.

a class period (Williams, 2018). Some assignments will demonstrate incremental learning during or between class periods, in the spirit of formative assessment; others will show a broader understanding of knowledge and skills, summative style. The teacher must decide what is most valuable in providing evidence of student learning. These work products (assessments) are prime candidates for grades that make it into the grade book.

Finally, take a moment to recognize that you are an educated, intelligent, caring, insightful, and resourceful professional who can and will make decisions about curriculum, assessment, and instruction effectively and meaningfully, no matter the noise out there. In the absence of leadership helping to define effective workflow practices, there are guideposts to consult, and you can find the way. Teaching is a people profession. Use your heart, intuition, and know-how to make the best decisions possible.

A True Story From Brooke

This is a funny but tragic story about grading. In my second year of teaching, I assigned a reading response journal that students completed three times a week for a quarter semester. This was a newly popular assessment tool in secondary education that sounded very promising in getting to know students' literary preferences and reading comprehension. I had students from four of my five classes—roughly 120 students—submit their journals at the end of the nine-week grading period. Period after period, students placed their work into stacks that grew into a mountain—as did the anxiety I felt from merely looking at the journals.

(Continued)

(Continued)

How was I possibly going to grade all of them? What feedback would I provide? What was the purpose of this assignment again? That afternoon, I loaded the trunk of my car with three plastic crates that carved red creases in my palms. I shut the lid and drove away into the winter night. Eventually, summer break came and I needed to sell my car. It wasn't until a prospective buyer wanted to look into the trunk did I realize what was in there—120 student reading journals. I stood staring, aghast at the denial or avoidance that brought me to this moment four months later. I felt shame, and was so embarrassed I could have died. Yes, I had forgotten all about the piles of composition books. And the kicker was that not a single student had asked about them—ever. Not a single one. To this day, I feel as though I should write each student an apology for wasting his or her time. The sad thing is they probably wouldn't recall the assignment, much less the lack of feedback. I learned an unforgettable lesson that day about the importance of meaningful work, informal assessment, and workflow. I promised myself that I would never place myself, or the students, in that bind again. If I wasn't clear about why I would be asking students to do work, and if I wouldn't be attending to it in a timely way, then it would be better not to assign it in the first place.

Patterns

People who work in or attend school have a concept of time that is different from those who don't. School people see time in the context of:

• Class periods	• Mid-quarters	• Bell schedules	• Vacations
• Contact time	• Trimesters	• Hiring cycles	• Government holidays
• Planning periods	• Semesters	• Budget cycles	• Fall = work
	• Block days		• Summer = break

This unique orientation to time informs a way of being in the world for both educators and students. Additionally, there is an overlay of seasonal and time changes, school calendaring, and various transitions that are all at play throughout the school year. It is helpful to look at the influence of these patterns as they relate to your self-care practices, because there are certain times of the year that will require more attention and structure than others. Remember Ms. Patel from the beginning of the chapter? Think about how transitioning back to school following a holiday vacation is different from transitioning into a new school year. What do you notice about yourself when winter approaches and daylight has disappeared by the time you leave the building for the day?

It is important to note that adolescents who live with chronic stress and trauma are impacted by these patterns as well. Transitions and lack of structure are difficult for students who are dysregulated to begin with. Like bustling winds that often accompany the fall season, students and teachers alike can feel unsettled and out of sorts at this time of year. Long winter days can trigger depressive episodes, and holiday breaks in unstable homes are not joyful or festive. Winter holidays may cause a resurfacing of grief and loss. What follows is a reminder of what is missing when a student's experience is not congruent with what our culture says holidays with family should be. The rigidity of the school schedule can be hard to adjust to after unstructured time during breaks.

There is often an increase of illness during the winter months, which leads to absences, which leads to increased stress when a student falls behind. As the long winter rolls into spring, there is an increase in anxiety as energy returns to the system. Time speeds up as students and teachers head into spring, knowing how much there is to do before the end of the year, especially for graduating seniors.

When it comes to the classroom, energy and stamina are also impacted by the patterns of the school year. This ebb and flow should inform when the best time of year is to engage in learning and assessment activities such as a highly involved, long-term project. Is there a stretch of time in the school calendar that will help cultivate momentum? Do students have the capacity to stay with it? Do you, as the teacher, have the capacity to facilitate and assess it? If there is limited time, then it may be best to either modify the assignment or identify a better time in the school year in order to reduce the panic created by running out of teaching days. Frequently, meaningful learning opportunities take longer than planned, so it's wise to build in more time than seems needed.

Sustainability

The practice of creating habits and rituals is important to creating behavior change. Creating new habits can be challenging. Your brain wants to create habits to save itself energy (Duhigg, 2012). It's going to do it anyway, so you might as well be an active creator in the habits you choose. Having some system of accountability, and surrounding yourself with people who support you, will help ensure you are successful in making the changes necessary for you to be vibrant and healthy. Shifting the focus from caring for others to caring for yourself is not easy or natural for teachers, so design a system that works for you. Figure 3.10 is an example of a self-care plan that is meant to be a springboard. Feel free to use this as a template or to design your own plan that will help you identify goals and stay on track. Be as creative or detailed as you would like.

Figure 3.10 Self-Care Plan

Include personally meaningful activities that support *you* to continue in your pursuit of self-regulation and balance. Good health involves adding something new and letting go of something that no longer serves you, in order to achieve balance. Think about how you might incorporate these activities both on the job and outside of work.

More of this . . .	Less of that . . .
Things That Bring Me Joy	Things That Drain My Energy
Relationships That Fulfill Me	Relationships That Exhaust Me
Ways to Move My Body	Ways I Stay Stuck
Rituals That Feed My Soul	Beliefs That Limit Me
Rituals to Help Me Transition Out of Work	
Affirmations: Messages of Positive Intentions and Values to State to Myself Every Day	
Heart Connection: What Are the Reasons I Became an Educator?	
Recovery: One Thing I Can Do to Restore Myself After a Really Hard Day	

Getting started can be the hardest part. Remember that sometimes you may need to build in more of something, while other times you may need to let go of something to create the right balance. Self-care plans are meant to be working, fluid, and interactive documents. Don't get stuck. Give yourself permission to modify, and adjust as frequently as needed. Figure 3.11 has some suggestions that might help spark ideas if getting started feels tough.

Figure 3.11   Forms of Self-Care

Leave work at work	Connect with non-school friends	Plan a vacation	Limit screen time
Mindfulness practices	Find a therapist	Connect with nature	Create quiet time for yourself
Say "no" more	Deep breathing	Make time for meaningful activities/hobbies	Exercise
Eat healthy	Ask for help	Journal (art, gratitude, writing, dreams)	Use a planner to protect self-care time/activities
Create art	Meditate	Say "yes" more	Create a vision board
Spiritual practices	Read non-work books	Take a class	Protect family time

Accountability Partners

Change is hard. In order to be successful, it is helpful to have an accountability partner or group. Accountability partners serve as gentle reminders to help you stay on track. The role of this person or group is to check in with you about your own process, as well as to encourage you. A good accountability partner is part drill sergeant and part cheerleader. Who in your life might be a good accountability partner? Is there a small group of people at your work or a coach who could fill that role?

Planning Habits for the Classroom

Winging it doesn't work, particularly if the aim is to mitigate stress and the effects of trauma. It does, however, create chaos and induce tension where there needn't be more. School days are characterized by plenty of unpredictability, which can be energizing in some instances, yet overall an ad hoc approach to planning only increases the likelihood of stress that further contributes to burnout.

The bell rings, and Mr. Johnson is desperately searching through his work bag for the day's lesson, while students impatiently watch his every move. Regretfully, he doesn't feel prepared. Finally, he locates it! He gives a small sigh of relief, although it's not the kind of plan he knows works best for his energetic and lively class. Today's topic is mitosis. He didn't make time to identify a student-centered activity in order to explore the topic, so he figures that he will just provide the students necessary information in a lecture format. What he doesn't cover in his lecture, he will have them read from their textbooks in class, then answer questions for homework. He really

(Continued)

(Continued)

doesn't like to lecture, but he has no other choice. Frazzled and hesitant, he begins, "Take out your notebooks, a pen, your textbook, and turn to page 12." Students sigh. And so it goes for 35 minutes . . . wah, wah, wah . . . and time drags on until the bell rings. Mr. Johnson is thankful that class is over. He is hoarse from talking at students, the students are numb from listening, and no one feels engaged or energized. The students drag themselves out the door and into the hall, where there is a noticeable increase in energy and conversation. Deflated and drained, Mr. Johnson sighs, wondering how he will muster up the energy to do this all again next period.

As an instructional coach, or fellow observer, surely you understand that it doesn't have to be this way. No one—neither Mr. Johnson nor his students—wants to repeat this lifeless pattern every day. In order to prevent this deadening effect, effective (and life-giving) planning habits are imperative, particularly those that place students at the center of the learning, where energy, interest, and engagement have a greater likelihood of increasing.

The Planning Habits Checklist (Figure 3.12) outlines an example of essential planning habits—in and outside of the classroom—that promote self-care in teachers and students. Take a moment to check in with yourself about what habits you have or would like to have in order to provide more care for yourself and your students.

Figure 3.12   Planning Habits Checklist

Elements of Effective Lesson Design (Behind the Scenes)	Elements of an Effective Teaching Mindset (Behind the Scenes)
❑ Anchored in content standards	❑ How am I doing?
❑ Student learning targets clearly defined (use of student-friendly language)	❑ Am I well-planned?
❑ Clearly defined rationale for learning (In other words, why are students learning this?)	❑ Am I calm? If not, what do I need to do to take care of myself?
❑ Warm-up/Do-Nows	❑ Am I feeling dread or anxiety? With what class? With whom? Why?
❑ Direct instruction, as needed	❑ Am I alert to those students who trigger me?
❑ Student-centered learning activities accompanied by student work (differentiated by content, work product, and process, as possible)	❑ Do I have a plan to relate with those students? A reset?
❑ Consideration for reteaching (anticipating confusion) and/or stretching learning	❑ Am I open to new possibilities?
❑ Formative assessment of student work throughout class period	❑ Am I loving?
❑ Exit Slip/Mastery Check	
❑ Plan for homework (practice from day's lesson)	

Taking Self-Care School-Wide

School leaders can help teachers identify strategies for determining what is most important in sustainable practice, then design systems to support them to get the work done effectively. Helping colleagues on the front line by supporting them in doing fewer things better—such as teaching fewer preps, taking a hiatus from coaching and from sponsoring clubs, and limiting supervisory duties—will help retain good teachers. This is not to mention guiding teachers in efficient workflow practices related to effective lesson planning and grading. Leadership entails preventing people from getting buried under the load. Never underestimate how much better it can make teachers feel about their work if they have permission to take on less in order to be more effective.

In thinking about school-wide professional growth in this area, it's understandable to wonder where, in an already packed calendar, school leadership can make the time to accommodate another topic for a faculty in-service, collaborative peer group, or whole-group learning experience. Figure 3.13 presents the case as to why self-care is an important practice to develop and sustain.

Figure 3.13   Why Administrators Should Care About Self-Care

Costs of Not Caring About It	Benefits of Caring About It
Poor health in teachers will impact students' safety/health/learning	Healthy staff and safe schools
Increase of staff out sick	Increased attendance
Low morale	Positive vibes abound
Lack of buy-in	Engagement in programming
Lack of productivity (staff meetings, attendance)	Increased productivity
Increased acting-out behaviors (not checking emails, poor planning and work quality)	Decreased acting-out behaviors
Energy drain	Energy flow
Time and money	Decreased staff turnover

Helping Teachers Help Themselves: The Role of School Leadership

Healthy, balanced teachers have a life outside of school. One of the ways that school leaders can support teachers in their own self-care process is to encourage work-life balance by taking time off when they are off, and providing time for teachers when they need to regroup. A simple strategy to support this idea is to encourage teachers not to assign work over school breaks. Students and teachers both need the time away. Reentry into the school routine can be taxing—even more so if teachers immediately face a pile of student work that needs to be graded. It never hurts to surprise the teachers with an early dismissal on those in-service days, thus providing them an opportunity to determine for themselves how to spend their time.

Nearly every teaching contract offers sick and personal days. As a school leader, consider encouraging faculty members to take a "mental health day" or other version of leave when just a little time away might offer refreshment and renewal. Leadership has the opportunity to create a school culture that upholds faculty well-being as necessary and required, not selfish or unprofessional. According to the U.S. Department of Education, 53% of public school leavers reported that general work conditions were better in their current position than they had been in teaching (NCES, 2014). Imagine if it were expected that teachers take care of themselves and were provided permission and the necessary resources to do so. Perhaps this shift in expectations would create better working conditions.

It is difficult to provide the requisite patience, clear thinking, warmth, and balance for the job when running on fumes. You cannot produce what you do not possess. In addition to regular school demands, colleagues are often pressed to put in extra time outside the classroom tutoring students, coaching athletes, or tending to a difficult student issue. Even writing college recommendations can be a source of pressure. Teachers are easily overworked and overwhelmed. These are ideal times to encourage one another to take a day to recharge.

Guiding teachers to home in on what matters most in designing curriculum, as we have done in this chapter, presents a leadership opportunity for you to give them license to do this thoughtful and courageous work. You can provide the support, and the necessary permission, for decision-making that emboldens them to implement a "less is more" philosophy. They need to know that they are trusted and will be supported in making decisions that are in the best interest of their students and of themselves.

Factors That Contribute to Teacher Well-Being

• Class size	• Work space
• Student load	• Duties outside of the classroom
• Number of course preps	• Quality human interactions and a sense of community
• Receiving positive feedback from one's supervisor	• Professional development on responding to adverse childhood experiences (ACEs)
• School safety plans	• Having fun together
• School discipline policy	• Family communication policies
• Grading practices/expectations	• Time-off policy and support
• Availability of instructional materials	• Stance toward state testing
• Choice in curriculum design	• Evaluation practices
• Common planning time	

Leading by Example: The Role of Self-Care in the Life of a Leader

If school leaders are frayed and running in all directions, it sends a signal that things are dysregulated and chaotic and perhaps there is cause for serious concern. A retired principal friend of ours once shared his wisdom, saying that all things roll down from the top. Whether stream, avalanche, mudslide, or stress: It all flows downhill. And where stress and trauma are concerned, the effect can be crushing. Doing nothing is not a sustainable model for taking care of members of our school communities.

If, as a school leader, you feel as though calm is out of reach, and more often than not you operate in crisis mode, ask yourself:

 What support might I need to care for myself?

 Do I have a relevant self-care plan in place?

 What changes can I make in order to experience more balance and well-being?

Caring for yourself and managing your stress—by saying "no," doing fewer things better, delegating, and having firm boundaries—sustains the wellness of those down the hill. The school leaders who have lasted and remain effective are those who model strong self-care practices, including an uncanny ability to prioritize, communicate, and share the joy of the work. This is not an easily acquired skill, because the demands on school leadership are many.

Reflections

The key to sustaining the effective work of teaching lies in being able to maintain your well-being. Only you can take care of you.

1. What might I need to say "no" to in order to say "yes" to my physical, emotional, and mental health?

____

____

____

2. What is my self-care plan? With whom can I share it?

____

____

____

(Continued)

(Continued)

3. What prevents me from taking care of myself?

____

____

____

4. What do I need from school leadership in order to do my job effectively and for the long haul?

____

____

____

Toolkit for Tomorrow

In an effort to cultivate self-care, tomorrow I can:

- ❏ increase awareness around the need to take care of myself physically, mentally, emotionally, and spiritually.
- ❏ identify the signs of burnout.
- ❏ name places where I can say "no."
- ❏ interact with colleagues who are energizing, positive, and supportive.
- ❏ develop a self-care plan and follow up with an accountability partner.
- ❏ assess where I can strive to uncover and discover curricular topics, in exchange for covering content.
- ❏ identify a workflow plan that is manageable and sustainable.
- ❏ get support from my instructional coach, administrator, or the school counselor in how to implement self-care.
- ❏ lead with compassion . . . for myself and for others.

In the End, Be Loving

You became a teacher because you wanted to make a difference in the lives of students. Incorporating self-care practices will allow you to thrive in the career you love—for longer. Commit to caring for yourself with energy, patience, and love. Make the time. Accept the challenge. Honor the commitment. You are worth it. Your students are worth it. You have too much invested in teaching to burn out.

Know Me to Teach Me

You can't motivate a student that you don't know.
—**Theodore Sizer**

Jason Falucci sits in his freshman math class, staring out the window. He is one of four Jasons in the freshman grade level. Jason V. sits two seats behind him. Jason F. is the youngest brother of Tom and Anthony Falucci; Tom is currently a senior at the same school, and Anthony graduated last year. Mr. Shea is a veteran teacher who has been at the school for 18 years and taught the older Faluccis. Mr. Shea's class doesn't have a seating chart. He allows students to sit where they want, as long as they are not disruptive. There is a fair amount of chaos and chatter as class begins, and Mr. Shea starts to talk while writing math problems on the board. Jason talks with his tablemate Elron, not realizing that class has begun. Mr. Shea turns to face the class and raises his voice: "Tom, stop talking!" Jason and Elron continue their conversation. "Tom! I asked you to stop talking!" Mr. Shea exclaims, while moving toward his desk to grab a detention slip. The boys continue to visit, as does the rest of the class. Mr. Shea walks over to Jason and slaps a detention slip down on his desk for disrespect. Confused and angry, Jason looks down at the slip, looks up at Mr. Shea, and says, "My name is not Tom," to which Mr. Shea replies, "You know what I meant, Falucci," before turning on his heels and walking back to the front of the room to continue his lecture.

Knowing Students Well: Why Is It Important?

Knowing students well is the predicate for being able to meet students' needs as learners. When you are able to know your students both as people and as learners, you can better target your instruction in order to support their growth and their pursuit of proficiency.

What does authentic connection between teachers and students look like? Humans are social creatures, hardwired for connection. We can't survive without it. Knowing your students (which doesn't mean needing to know the details of their private lives or their traumatic experiences) is a foundational piece of relationship building. Mr. Shea might ask, "What's in a name?" Ask any parent who named his or her child. Names hold incredible power and meaning. Knowing a person starts with knowing his or her name and using it—not making up a nickname, not shortening the name because you can't pronounce it, but making every available effort to call students by the names they identify with. If you are not sure, then ask them. Not doing so will cause a student to shut down and disconnect from you, because it feels disrespectful. In fact, it is the quickest way to lead a person to assume you don't care about him or her. That's not your intent. You are in this profession to connect with kids and make a difference. This chapter highlights ways to really know students as individual learners and the unique challenges of working with kids who have suffered chronic stress and trauma.

Student Experience

As discussed in Chapter 1, an adolescent's primary developmental task is identity formation. Kids are trying to figure out who they are and how they fit or don't fit into their environment. Their sense of self may be different from day to day; their ideology, values, and beliefs all can change on a whim. Parents and educators who spend most of their days with teens can get whiplash trying to keep up. It is *because* kids are constantly trying to figure out who they are that it is so important for you to know them. If this seems confusing, it is. Identity formation is fraught with many tensions for both teens and adults to navigate. Figure 4.1 highlights some of the tensions students feel when it comes to being seen and known by you.

Figure 4.1   Mixed Messages From the Mind of a Teenager

1. I want to be seen, yet I don't want to be seen.
2. I want to fit in, yet I don't want to stand out.
3. I know it all, yet I know nothing.
4. I want to be heard, yet I don't want to talk.
5. I want to be validated/valued, yet I don't want affirmation.

Students with chronic stress and trauma are not used to being seen, validated, respected, or truly known. They may be more apt to reject a teacher's efforts to compliment or affirm them. It isn't that they don't want it, but that it feels uncomfortable because it is unfamiliar and therefore may be perceived as untrustworthy. They also might make inappropriate efforts to be seen, by acting in ways that earn them not a positive response but rather angry, punitive, or other negative responses from adults.

Adult Experience

How can you know someone who doesn't know themselves? It can be frustrating, as an educator who teaches 150 students in a day, to try to "know" all the kids. There is a tension—because you are supposed to know them, supervise them, and engage them in a learning process, all while they are developing and trying to know themselves. It is also challenging because there is a fine line to walk between knowing a student and *not* knowing all the details of their personal life or history. Yet teachers must manage to get to know their students well enough for purposes of report cards, conferences, and so on—while fulfilling all the other requirements of the job, too.

Knowing kids may seem impossible when you have large student loads. Striking the balance between knowing *something* about each student and feeling like you have to know *everything* about all your students can be challenging. Here are some ideas to consider as you seek to connect with students in an authentic way.

Foundation for Effective Practice #1: Listen

When people feel heard, they feel seen and known. Listening—really listening, not rushing, not pushing your agenda, but really taking the time to hear what your students are saying (or not saying)—is critical when working with adolescents. Brenda Ueland wrote: "When we are listened to, it creates us, makes us unfold and expand. Ideas actually begin to grow within us and come to life" (1992). Slowing down, making eye contact, and paraphrasing what you heard are all great ways to let a student know you are deeply listening.

Foundation for Effective Practice #2: Provide Choices

Giving traumatized students choices is crucial. Obviously, providing choices will help with student engagement, but it also helps kids sift and sort out identity issues. Having choices empowers students who are powerless in other areas of their lives to exercise some measure of control and self-efficacy. Giving students choices whenever possible is also trust-building for the relationship. Through your actions, they will see that you trust them to make decisions that impact their learning and development. And this trust creates safety, helping them to take more risks to show themselves and be known by you and their classmates.

Foundation for Effective Practice #3: Trust Their Wisdom

Each of us is an expert in our own life. No matter how old or how young someone is, he or she is the only one who knows what it is like to live his or her life. Teens love to be experts. Even though, as an adult, you have years more experience, knowledge, and—don't forget—critical-thinking skills, don't underestimate the deep wisdom that comes from the hearts and minds of teenagers.

What Works in the Classroom: Knowing Students Well

In our experience, the average teacher spends approximately nine hours a day at school, of which approximately eight hours are with children. This does not include time spent coaching, tutoring, sponsoring, coordinating, chaperoning, or leading outside of the classroom. By any measure, this is a lot of time spent in relationship with adolescents. Additionally, with students coming and going in increments of 40 to 60 minutes a day (multiple times a day), developing and staying in strong and healthy relationships can be a challenge. There is simply not enough time to know each student, let alone assess his or her level of understanding . . . unless you look at how you can create a smaller scale whereby you interact with students in more accessible and effective ways. Waving a magic wand to reduce class size—and, perhaps, shorten or lengthen the school period or day—would be great. However, you have to find ways of working within the system that currently exists.

Meet Ruby. Ruby, an eighth-grader, doesn't consider herself a "good" student. She remembers struggling since third grade with reading and writing concepts, particularly those embedded within difficult texts across all content areas. She is a slow reader and takes extra time and energy to comprehend what she reads in any subject. Her struggle is partly attributed to changing schools frequently, and those she has been in for a year or more have had problems of their own. In fact, she had five different language arts teachers in her seventh-grade year alone.

The first day of class in eighth grade, she shared that she didn't feel confident in her literacy skills—a characteristic that her social studies teacher, Ms. George, learned through a brief intro survey that she gives to each student. The questions include: (1) What is your formal name? What name do you prefer that I call you? (2) How would you describe your experience as a student in general? As a reader and a writer? (3) What do you want me to know about how you learn that will help you achieve in this class?

On any given day in Ms. George's class, students work in small table groups. Every day, each student is expected to participate in reading and problem-solving activities related to questions in the textbook or within a project-based learning activity. Ruby was placed in a group of three other students, whose names and interests she learned the first day of school through an "ice breaker" activity. She will have the option to work with a different group of students after the middle of the quarter, but for now she will develop her cooperative learning skills with the same group of students.

On a particular day, students have been asked to begin a project-based learning unit entitled, "Where Is the Line Between 'Primitive Society' and 'Civilization?'" (MyPBLWorks, n.d.). Ruby and her team work to tackle the first step of the project. Ms. George uses cooperative learning structures to help students to define their role in group participation (in order to minimize the "free rider" effect), whereby each student has a specific, while equitable, role to play within a group context. In this case, the group of four fulfills roles such as timekeeper, materials manager, project record keeper, and spokesperson. Each student will have a turn at fulfilling and reflecting on each of the roles. This clarity is helpful to Ruby, because her past experiences with small-group work left her frustrated and feeling like the workload was unfairly borne by the few who "cared."

Assessment Format

Ms. George uses a small-group instructional model, for two reasons: (1) for students to actively participate in their learning and that of their peers and (2) for the teacher to learn more about *individual* student learning. Neither of these outcomes is possible without a structure that fosters student conversation with one another or with their teacher. Fortunately, Ms. George capitalizes on the opportunity provided through small-group models to listen intently. In fact, one of her main methods of assessment is conferring. She pulls up a chair next to the student from whom she wants to hear. She regularly asks students to share a piece of work that they have been focusing on that day or over the past couple of days. Examples typically include written evidence of learning, such as an opinion piece or a summary, a reading response, a reflection on their problem-solving process, project conclusions, and self-reflection of performance tasks. Formative assessments—ongoing, authentic feedback, such as these—give students an opportunity to show what they are thinking (Tovani, 2011). Ms. George's goal for student conferring is simply to know more about what a particular student knows or doesn't know about any given topic or concept and to provide targeted instruction, a high-leverage instructional strategy in moving understanding forward. It's where the "magic" happens (Serravallo, 2019). Ms. George's conferring protocol consists of four steps, outlined in Figure 4.2.

Figure 4.2   Conferring Steps

Conferring Steps and Purpose	Student Role	Teacher Role
Step 1: Clarity of Learning Goal	Asks self and explains: "What do I understand the purpose of this [assessment] to be?"	Listens and takes notes Seeks clarification
Step 2: Evidence of Learning	Asks and explains: "What in this piece of my work specifically tells me that I understand what is expected of me to understand?" Explains: "This is where I am having difficulty. This is why I think I am stuck."	Listens and takes notes Seeks clarification by asking "Say more?" "Can you point to specifically what makes you think that?" "What is making this difficult for you?" "Where do you find yourself getting stuck?"
Step 3: Student Reflection paired with Teacher Targeted Instruction	Asks and explains: "What can I do to understand [this] better? Here might be some ways that you could help me."	Asks self and provides: "What instruction can further this student's understanding?" Asks student: "How might I be able to help you better understand and to do?"
Step 4: Learning Plan	Explains: My learning and next steps based on this conversation and my work.	Explains: My steps to follow up with you as a result of our conversation.

In order to help herself keep track of each student's learning within the conferring model, she maintains an online spreadsheet that she fills out on her tablet as she sits with students. She has tried several methods of recordkeeping over the years. Regardless of the method, recording their input and her thinking formalizes the conference, helps her keep track of whom she meets with in her rotation, and indicates the launching point for the next conference.

Ruby, who has never had this level of involvement in her own learning assessment, has had to grow in both (1) her skill of talking with her teacher in this manner and (2) her own awareness as a learner. She will let you know that she likes being asked about her learning. She thinks she may actually like Ms. George's class . . . because she feels successful in it.

Homework and Grades

The needs of students experiencing the effects of chronic stress and trauma are often a poor fit with standard homework and grading policies. Instability can lead to sporadic attendance, paired with fluctuating performance. Ms. George's school has in place a policy that allows her to take both late classwork and homework within a week or more. Figure 4.3 provides details of her communication with students about her policies.

Figure 4.3   Ms. George's Homework and Grading Policies

Homework is about practice. I will be providing you opportunities to practice your learning and develop your understanding throughout this course. My policy follows that of our school.

My policy is as follows:
- Students should submit their homework on the assigned due date; however,
  - If you are absent, please plan on submitting it as soon as you return to school. If you find that you cannot do so, please communicate with me as soon as possible. There is always a way through a homework dilemma.
  - If you are unable to attend to your homework for another reason, please communicate with me, and we will devise a plan for make-up work. I don't need to know all the details as to why you were unable to submit your work, yet I do need for us to identify a plan to complete it.

Grading policies assign value to your work, so that you can earn a grade in the grade book and on your progress report. Of all the things I know about you, grades are only a small and formal aspect of who you are as a student and as a person. My policy follows that of our school.

My policy is as follows:
- Students will be given grades on their work according to the requirements and success criteria provided. If the assignment is unclear, please communicate with me. Your success is my success.
- The school's grading scale is as follows: A = 90–100, B = 89–80, C = 79–70, D = 69–60, F = 59 or below.
- Should you disagree with grades given by me, let's identify a time to discuss the matter. I would like there to be a shared understanding of the grade.

Typically with larger assignments, students are asked to join Ms. George for an additional instructional session during lunch or an off-period. The policy is clearly stated from the first days of school. Students are asked to communicate with her, or any teacher, as a means of self-advocating, which is a long-term goal of student independence.

Grading policies are created not to punish, but rather to promote competency. They offer students insight into their own performance relative to standards and success criteria. If it takes several attempts, sometimes with additional instruction, then that is what is necessary. Students who are not accustomed to policies that require a certain degree of persistence may struggle at first. Several times, in our experience, we've observed students who would rather just take the "F" and move on. They don't know any other strategy for getting through the course. Sadly, the cost of *moving on* is a lack of competency (i.e., understanding the material). Students cannot afford to lose the opportunity to acquire the skills and knowledge needed to deepen their minds, navigate the world, and develop a sense of efficacy as learners.

The Art of Listening

An important feature of Ms. George's practice is that she is an excellent listener. She has made it an important feature of her instructional repertoire by intentionally honing her skills over the years. It has not come easily, since she did not have a model to build from. When she was a student herself, most of her teachers delivered content through lecture. She was not asked to talk about her understanding of concepts or skills; rather, she was tested on discrete units of learning through weekly quizzes and unit tests. Talking to her teacher about her understanding through the examination of her work would have been about as foreign to her as selecting her own topic of research.

Active listening requires a heightened sense of self-awareness. It requires the listener to ask questions like these: "What am I hoping for in this conversation?" "What is my motivation?" "Am I hoping to hear something in particular?" "Am I open to other ideas?" In student conferences, it's helpful to be patient and wait for the learner to do the work of reflection, analysis, and naming. Cornelius Minor (2019) reminds us that, as teachers, "our superpower is listening" (p. 11).

Knowing oneself as a listener is important to recognizing what might trigger certain behaviors that prevent *powerful listening*. Figure 4.4 lists some stumbling blocks that prevent effective listening. As you review each one of them, identify a possible solution that would support your best listening practices within a teaching and learning situation.

Figure 4.4   Stumbling Blocks to Effective Listening

Block: Interrupting the speaker

Solution: ______________________

Block: Providing advice too quickly

Solution: ______________________

Block: Thinking about your response while the speaker is speaking

Solution: ______________________

Block: Being uncomfortable with silence

Solution: ______________________

Block: Bringing your own agenda to the conversation

Solution: ______________________

Source: Adapted from Sweeney and Harris (2020). *The Essential Guide for Student-Centered Coaching: What Every Coach and School Leader Needs to Know.*

Trusting Them

Students tell us, as teachers, what we need to know. They know what it's like to be adolescents living in modern times, struggling to grow up under the stress of expectations, biological change, technology, and social tensions. They can speak most insightfully to *their* experiences. They offer solutions to problems of which we are not even aware as adults living life from a different perspective. They have amazing, unique, funny, creative, original, problem-solving, and splendid ideas. When given the opportunity to talk, students can speak astutely to what they like, what they don't like, what interests them, what causes fear, what creates boredom, and so on. Most important, we can trust them to put forth ideas that will advance our shared goals, such as how to best teach them in order for them to learn. To return to Ms. George, underlying her pedagogy is her belief that students can be trusted to know who they are and what they need. Often a good teacher simply needs to know how to nudge their thinking and help students name what they already know, and what to do as a result.

One practical exercise is to offer students the ability to name their own goals for the course, the school year, and their education on the whole. Frequently students just haven't had the opportunity to name for themselves what they hope for out of situations they encounter in school. Naming goals, and the steps needed to take to achieve them, is a concrete aspect of developing self-efficacy. Imagine utilizing a simple goal-setting exercise as part of a student's coursework. Figure 4.5 provides a template for this type of goal-setting.

Figure 4.5   Student Goal-Setting

Student Input	Teacher Input
Name:	Name:
My goal(s) for the class is to: _______________________ ____	
I plan to achieve this goal by: Step 1: _________________________________ Step 2: _________________________________ Step 3: _________________________________	
I need to be aware of the following possible obstacle(s) to my achieving my goal: Possible obstacle(s): _________________________________	
I have made progress in the following ways: 1. _________________________________ 2. _________________________________ 3. _________________________________	
I will seek the following resources and people to support me in reaching my goal: _________________________________ _________________________________ _________________________________	

Using a process to set goals forges the way for follow-up conversations between student and teacher that cultivates trust, support, and accountability. Here are some questions to think about related to building trust:

▶ *How would I explain the trust I have in my students?*

▶ *What makes me doubt them?*

▶ *What can I do to increase my trust in students? What practices foster trust?*

You may be hesitant to defer to students in their learning if you haven't yet seen the benefits that it provides in your planning, instruction, and assessment practices. Trust us; it's similar to locating the last piece of the puzzle that defines an entire picture.

Taking Knowing Others School-Wide

Know names. Knowing students well across an entire school building can be challenging, given the sheer number of students in some schools. Learning cultures that do personalization well place an emphasis on knowing students by their names—including correct pronunciation and spelling—and recognizing personal (asset-driven) characteristics about students. Placing emphasis on student assets—such as their interests, talents, skills, and personality—makes for joyful starting points, particularly with students experiencing chronic stress or trauma. Many of these students who live on the margins go unnoticed and show up on the radar for indicators of concern. Knowing their detention records, absentee statistics, learning limitations, family crises, deprivations, or failure rates is not a positive starting point; these are elements of only part of their stories.

> **Consider the following questions as you build your practice in *knowing* students:**
>
> - What is one current system in your school to help adults—teachers, administration, and support staff—acknowledge students by name?
> - How can you know students' names within the first couple weeks of school?
> - Can you name something positive about each one of them? If not, how can you work toward this goal?
> - In a large school, what support systems—such as classrooms, advisory programs, and clubs—promote the fact that at least one adult knows a particular student well?

Everyone wants to be known for what they do well. Often students who have trouble in school are known only for the challenges they present. School leaders have tremendous opportunities to scratch the surface to reveal for students the good things that each one brings to the table.

Diversity, equity, and inclusion. We are living in both an exciting and a provocative era of education. In addition to major advances in brain research related to teaching and learning, we are exploring the impact of diversity, inclusion, and equity in the work of schools and learning organizations. Zaretta Hammond's work in *Culturally Responsive Teaching and the Brain* (2015) explains the powerful connection between culture and its impact on the brain as one significant factor in a student's development—a worthy and critical aspect of supporting individual students.

While human potential is limitless, fundamental concepts like culture and equity force each of us to unearth our assumptions and beliefs related to our own experiences—the good, the challenging, and the messy. The resulting vulnerability needed to explore our experiences, and those of others, offers school leaders an opportunity to think differently about how we invite students into their learning and their places of learning. Caveat: No one has it figured out. In fact, the braver you are in pursuing your understanding of each of these concepts, the more complicated the journey becomes. The point is to persist in your understanding, whatever your role. Schools offer a particular opportunity to cultivate cultures of trust, safety, and grace in order to investigate our individual and collective journeys. The goal is to understand . . . and, basically, to love students for all of their differences.

> **In exploration of diversity, equity, and inclusion, consider asking the following questions:**
>
> - How does your school approach the varying experiences of each member of the school community?
> - Is there inclusion even if there is diversity?
> - How do your curriculum and materials mirror your various learners? How might they do so better?
> - Is there equity even if there is diversity? How might your approach to instruction address the needs of each learner?
> - What resources out there can assist you and your team in leading discussions about diversity, equity, and inclusion?

Education offers each of us not only an exploration of what makes us tick as individuals (family origin, socioeconomic status, race, learning abilities, language, religion, gender, etc.), but also an opportunity to peek into what makes others who they are as a result of their experiences. Teachers offer the lead in this exploration.

Personalization. Sometimes in the onslaught of demands on those in leadership positions, it's easy to lose focus on the people that compose the organization. Fostering a healthy school culture that values people points to leadership that prioritizes individuals and their particular contributions to the school community, while keeping a focus on the purpose of the organization: to educate young people—with everything that entails.

Since people are at the heart of this work, it's easier to focus on the people in school contexts that are of human scale (Toch, 1991). Individuals are more easily seen, heard, and recognized in settings that lend themselves to seeing, hearing, and recognizing people more readily; in this regard, scale matters, and of course it matters for students in trauma even more so. By defining professional learning communities, Richard DuFour and Robert Eaker (1998) gave education a structure for bringing together small groups of practitioners in order to focus more intently on individual and collective student need—a welcome practice in pursuit of identifying students with effective interventions and practices. Advisory programs, schools within schools, and small high schools continue to provide a more personalized learning environment. These environments impact adolescents in a positive way, and they are particularly helpful for students who are dealing with the effects of stress and trauma. Smaller structures allow you, as a leader, to focus more intently on each person within your school. Knowing them—both students and teachers—enables you to best serve them through responsible policies and practices.

Here are some questions for you to consider in cultivating personalization:

- Is knowing individuals well a priority of school leadership? If not, how might it become so?
- How might the school be brought "down to human scale" through programming and structure, primarily for the student experience?
- How might systems and structures help adults, particularly those in leadership positions, know other adults well?

Finally, as will be discussed in Chapter 5, it can be challenging to balance knowing people well and maintaining healthy boundaries. As with students and teachers in a classroom, providing clarity of role and purpose assist individuals in identifying appropriate behavior. There is a tension between work life and personal life; one influences the other. Leading people in relationship-based organizations requires ongoing attention to personalization—not an easy task, but one that is important to building the foundation for learning.

Reflections

Understanding your students' identity is an essential aspect of providing quality learning experiences for them. Students respond best to those adults who recognize them as individuals, with their unique strengths and challenges.

1. What do I need to know about students in order to best teach them and for them to learn? What *don't* I need to know?

____

____

____

2. What prevents me from knowing my students well?

____

____

____

3. What system or structure can assist me in learning their names and asset-driven characteristics?

____

____

____

4. What do I need from school leadership in order to offer a more personalized education to my students?

____

____

____

5. How can I be better known by my peers and administration?

____

____

____

Toolkit for Tomorrow

In an effort to know students well, tomorrow I can:

- ❏ know each student by name and at least one asset he or she possesses.
- ❏ be aware of their interests, strengths, and passions.
- ❏ engage students through relevant and responsive curriculum.
- ❏ trust students to know themselves.
- ❏ build listening into my assessment practices.
- ❏ find times in the day to slow down and connect with students.
- ❏ lead with compassion . . . for myself and for others.

In the End, Be Loving

To truly be known by others is something all humans desire. Schools can provide unique opportunities for students to feel valued and loved. It takes intention and attention to bring to life this important aspect of education. What you do matters in the life of children—all children, especially those who deal with burdens you can neither see nor imagine.

Healthy Relationships in Complicated Times

Boundaries define us. They define what is me and is not me. A boundary shows me where I end and someone else begins, leading me to a sense of ownership. Knowing what I am responsible for gives me freedom.

—Henry Cloud

Mr. Valence sits alone in his classroom after school. He stares at the pile of math homework, wondering how he will get it all done. He glances at the clock and notices he has only a few minutes before cross-country practice starts, and he resigns himself to the fact that he'll be late, again. *It's okay*, he thinks to himself, *the kids know how to start warm-ups without me*. He continues to grade while ruminating on the fact that he has to get the report he promised to complete, as part of committee work, to the AP before 6:30 tonight. Meanwhile, his wife is expecting him for dinner with her folks at 6:00. He looks up to see a student, Jenny, standing in the doorway. She approaches without knocking and says, "Hey, can I talk to you?" while plopping down in the chair across from him. Jenny is one of his favorite students. She participates in class and has an outgoing personality. Visibly upset, Jenny continues: "I need some advice. My mom is so pissed at me because I snuck out to meet my boyfriend at a party last night, and now she says I can't see him anymore. She is so mad, I don't want to go home. She is totally overreacting. I mean, I am 15 years old. What do you think I should do?" Mr. Valence feels flattered that Jenny trusts him enough to ask for advice, so he throws out some ideas that might possibly help her. He knows that he is now officially very late for practice, but he doesn't want Jenny to feel like he doesn't care, so he sits for 20 more minutes with her, alone, in his classroom, before they both head down to cross-country practice. As they enter the gym together, another student turns to her friend and whispers something, and they both laugh.

Healthy Relationships: Why Are They Important?

Relationships are complicated, especially in secondary schools. As social beings, humans are driven by a desire to connect, commune, and collaborate. We believe that healthy relationships are foundational for learning both inside and outside the classroom. Clear boundaries, communication, trust, and positive regard are essential for fostering healthy school culture among all stakeholders. When poor boundaries exist, people get hurt.

If people, especially in positions of power, are not held accountable to act like responsible adults, then students, the school, and educators' careers are at risk. It is the responsibility of the adult to act like an adult professional (not a friend, nor a parent). School communities may *feel* like families, which can be amazing, healing, and inspiring; this is why it is the responsibility of every adult member of the school to be reflective when it comes to wrestling with the questions put forth in this chapter. It is not the student's job to meet the emotional needs of the adult—that is something the adult must do for himself or herself. If hard conversations about creating healthy boundaries at your school are not happening, they should be. Figure 5.1 lists some of the risks associated with poor boundaries.

Figure 5.1 Potential Consequences of Poor Boundaries

- Resentment
- Insecurity
- Ethical dilemmas
- Feeling embarrassed
- Feeling ashamed
- Unintended consequences
- Abuse
- Feeling unsafe
- Breach of trust
- Confusion
- Paralysis

- Unintentionally sending the wrong message
- Failure
- Social isolation (not having adult friends outside of school)
- Taking your work home (ruminating about work or students)
- Irritability
- Not attending to daily tasks
- Working too much or too little
- Secrecy

Student Experience

Kids who have experienced multiple adverse childhood experiences (ACEs) probably have not been raised with clear expectations and boundaries. Sometimes limits are not set at all. Other times, lines get drawn and then erased, are invisible, or feel like barbed wire. Often kids don't know they crossed a line until it's too late and they are in trouble. Messages from caregivers may be unclear—for example, silent treatment is deployed instead of healthy communication. When there is a conflict, kids are expected to "just figure it out" and are confused by the ambiguity of the ever-changing "rules." And sadly, some kids have suffered abuse, in which their physical and/or emotional boundaries have been shattered.

For these students, living in chaotic environments where trust has been broken and expectations are elusive, healthy relationships are uncharted territory. The kids can't find their own edges, the lines are blurred, and they need your help to set appropriate limits so they might grow in this regard. We all do better when expectations and roles are clearly defined. Can you see how Mr. Valence may be getting into a sticky situation with Jenny?

Adult Experience

Boundary disturbances show up in classrooms in well-intentioned but slippery ways. One tension identified earlier is the need to connect with your students while maintaining your role. Creating connection and safety often includes some measure of vulnerability and sharing on the part of the teacher. How do you know the right formula? How much is too much? When is it appropriate to share a personal story or to ask a personal question of a student? Sharing personal stories is a normal way to connect with students and colleagues: It's a way to be seen as the unique person you are. Eric Jensen suggests sharing a 60-second vignette about yourself each week as a way to connect with students (Jensen, 2013). Telling funny stories, sharing your experience, and highlighting your passion can help students see you as an individual, not just a teacher; however, sharing a *deeply personal* story with students would be an example of crossing a healthy boundary.

In addition to sharing your own personal stories as a way to connect, it may also feel really good when a student "trusts" you enough to share what is going on in his or her life. Although, like Mr. Valence, in some way you may be pleased to find yourself in the role of confidant, you may also be putting yourself and the student at risk. So, in these situations, we recommend you model appropriate self-disclosure by helping the student "contain" his or her story while you remain present to him or her. Students shouldn't have to share their traumas to feel known or to connect with others, and they may not know better. Educators should not draw out traumatic stories from students (even when students are more than willing to share) in order to feel more compassionate or connected.

Although Mr. Valence may *be* trustworthy, that doesn't mean it is within his role as a math teacher to act as confidant. As a someone who is required by law to report suspicions of abuse, self-harm, and harm to others, his poor boundary-setting opens him up to liability should Jenny's safety be at risk and he is unsure how to respond. A better choice for Mr. Valence, first, would be to have explicit office hours and to close his door when office hours are over. He could also establish a more public environment in which to provide support. This could prevent students from popping in after hours when he is alone after school.

However, once Jenny started sharing, the more appropriate response may have been to express his concern for her while redirecting her to the appropriate resource—a school counselor, an administrator, or a resource officer. This could sound something like the following: "Wow, Jenny, it sounds like things are hard for you right now. Although I want to support you, I think it's best that you check in with Ms. Angel—because, as your math teacher, I am not really comfortable or qualified to support you with this personal issue. I am going to walk you to her office so that you two can talk more." A statement like this is a win-win, because Mr. Valence is able to maintain his professionalism while providing appropriate support to Jenny. Mr. Valence needs to connect with other adults in the building to best support Jenny. Who are the adults in your building whom you can ask for help when you are concerned about a student (whether during the day or at night)?

Foundation for Effective Practice #1: Defining Boundaries

There are confusing tensions that exist in schools, making it difficult to know what appropriate and healthy relationships look like in the classroom, in the building, and with families of students. For adults, this landscape is hard enough to navigate, but for teenagers who are impacted by chronic stress and trauma it can feel extremely disorienting and confusing. Kids want to connect. They want to be seen and to have your approval. And kids who have experienced a higher number of ACEs most likely have not had appropriate relationships modeled for them. For many such kids, relationships are absent of consistency, trust, and clarity, yet full of boundary violations, mixed messages, and unspoken expectations. Becoming more comfortable holding the tension between two opposing needs (need to connect + need to stay in your role) will help you maintain boundaries with students and coworkers.

Boundaries come in many forms—some are visible and some invisible. There are two main types of boundaries: physical and emotional. Physical limits are defined by your skin (body), whereas emotional limits are dependent on your age, your roles, your relationships with those around you, your requirements for safety, and your choices about how you want to be treated (Katherine, 1991).

Healthy relationships are dependent on your ability to manage relational boundaries, including your emotions, your reactions, saying "no," and attending to your own emotional "backyard." No matter what form the boundaries take, they exist to help you define and clarify your personal responsibility and your sense of autonomy over yourself. Clear boundaries help answer questions like "What am I responsible for attending to?" "What can I control, and what is out of my control?" "How is our relationship mutually defined?" How do boundaries impact your classroom management, planning, and engagement?

Boundaries are about identifying the literal and metaphorical *fences* that surround your *self*, so that you may be responsible for what is on your side of the fence. That is not to say you don't care about your "neighbors," but by creating and maintaining healthy boundaries (made by you and for you) first, you will create safety and clarity. Having done that, you can better negotiate relationships with students, colleagues, and parents.

Set clear expectations. Having transparent and direct communication will help students know they can trust you to be reliable and appropriate. They will also feel respected, and so will you.

Foundation for Effective Practice #2: Creating Awareness

Creating awareness and self-reflection is always a great place to start. Here are some basic reflection questions to help you start to notice if you are experiencing some boundary disturbances. This awareness usually starts in your gut. When something *feels* uncomfortable, confusing, or wrong, that is usually a clue that there is a boundary disturbance. *Trust your gut.* Questions such as the following can help you gauge your gut feeling about situations that might threaten your boundaries.

▶ *What is it about this student/interaction that triggers me?*

▶ *Why does this situation feel uncomfortable?*

▶ *With whom can I consult?*

▶ *Why am I feeling so angry/frustrated/upset/powerless?*

Students with trauma need you to be clear, especially when they themselves are not. Figure 5.2 lists some warning signs of poor boundaries or boundary disturbances. It is meant to highlight the potential gray areas that signal a need to pay more attention to your practices. As with everything, creating awareness about your practice is the best way to know whether you need to make a shift (or help someone else make a shift).

Figure 5.2 Warning Signs That Your Boundaries May Be Eroding

- Inconsistent policy enforcement (making exceptions for some students and not others)
- Noticing the types of students you connect with easily as well as the ones that really challenge you, and *why*
- Extending your hours for some students and not others
- Avoiding certain students or wanting to spend more time with certain students
- Sharing inappropriate personal stories
- Poor classroom management
- Private meetings with students outside of normal meeting times
- Thinking/worrying about students outside of school
- Spending too much time at school or at school-related functions
- Burnout symptoms (refer to Chapter 3)
- Poor self-care
- Working in isolation more than working in community

Foundation for Effective Practice #3: Setting Limits

As a loving and dedicated educator, you are in this business to connect with and make a difference to kids. Everyone comes with their own history and orientation to relationships, as well as their own awareness of the importance of setting boundaries. Understanding and creating boundaries can be challenging, even scary at first, especially if you have not had appropriate boundaries modeled for you. One example of a simple and powerful boundary-setting strategy is to say "no." If you're one of those people for whom saying "no" is hard, you are not alone. Saying "no" is a seemingly easy, but profoundly difficult, thing for many helping professionals to do. That's because asserting yourself to set a limit can feel uncomfortable or even scary. You might feel guilty, or you might fear angering the other person. Whenever you set a boundary, the person with whom you are setting it with may have a negative reaction (*external reaction*), as when a child who is refused candy throws a tantrum; there is also an *internal reaction*, an emotional reaction that you feel. If you fear the other person's potential reaction, or that he or she will perceive you negatively, it can be enough to keep you from even trying to set appropriate limits. Figure 5.3 shows several common emotional reactions among people when they think about saying "no."

Figure 5.3   Common Emotional Reactions to Limit-Setting

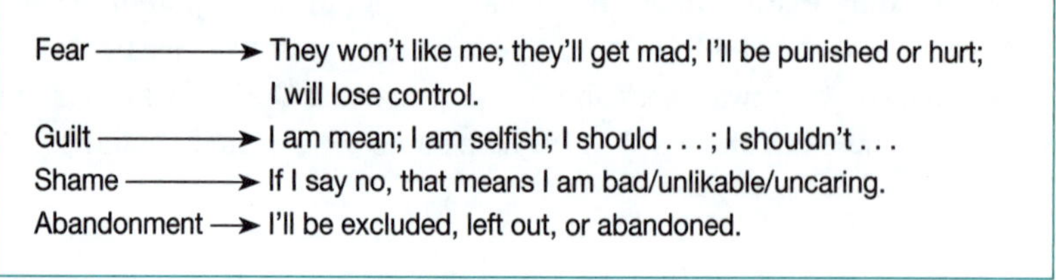

The good news is that learning to create healthy boundaries is totally possible. All it takes is awareness and practice, practice, practice. The more you practice, the more you'll see that you can tolerate these uncomfortable feelings and that people will respond to your requests as long as you hold the line. And if they don't, that is okay, because you are not responsible for their feelings or behavior. Setting boundaries doesn't make you cold, uncaring, or inflexible. It is about being realistic in terms of what you can control and what you choose to tolerate . . . on your side of the fence.

And if you're one of the people for whom saying "no" is easy, please understand that not everyone is there yet. As a coworker or leader in the school, you can help the people around you by increasing your awareness of the issue and by looking for signs that they may be having trouble saying "no" or setting limits. Back to Mr. Valence—he seems to have difficulty saying "no" based on the fact that he is overscheduled, isn't meeting his deadlines, or isn't fulfilling his professional and personal responsibilities.

He has spread himself too thin and probably isn't feeling effective or good about his performance—not to mention he seems to lack awareness of the mess he may be stepping into with his student Jenny. How might a colleague start a supportive conversation with Mr. Valence to help him increase his awareness about his boundary disturbances?

Foundation for Effective Practice #4: Accepting Personal Responsibility

Setting healthy boundaries requires accepting personal responsibility for your emotions, thoughts, and actions. Being accountable and responsible for your side of the fence enables you to move through life and relationships in a healthy way. When a person is not taking responsibility for his or her own emotions, thoughts, and feelings, things get messy. Feeling as though you lack autonomy and control over your*self* is a fast track to blaming others, feeling powerless, resentment, stress, guilt, and becoming overwhelmed. When you are working with adolescents who have experienced chronic stress and trauma, creating safety and trust requires clarity, consistency, and love. Once this foundation is established, the learning can begin.

What Works in the Classroom: Cultivating Healthy Relationships

Increasing your awareness and utilizing self-reflective practices are first steps in developing an internal compass that will guide your relationships with students. Next, let's look at how boundaries, role clarity, curriculum design, and collegial support can assist teachers in cultivating healthy school relationships.

Navigating Physical and Emotional Boundaries

Like Mr. Valence, teachers can't always anticipate what situations they'll find themselves in while working with children. Since educators are led by their care for children, it's likely they will experience uncomfortable circumstances in which students naturally are seeking connection with a person they trust.

Although great relationships are at the foundation of an effective teaching and learning community, it can be tricky when roles, and subsequently boundaries, aren't clearly defined. *Clarity* in task, learning intentions, and success criteria is paramount in order for students to be successful (Almarode & Vandas, 2018). Furthermore, clarity within roles and boundaries for both teachers and students—whether in the classroom, on the basketball court, on a field trip, in advisory, or at a dance—is critical for healthy relationships to flourish. The following story provides an example of how a lack of clarity can lead to confusion and conflict.

Miguel enters the classroom looking unusually defeated. Mrs. Howard detects his distress by the way that he slumps his shoulders, drags his feet, and refuses to look up when she says hello. Mrs. Howard wonders to herself why he is so upset. She resolves to focus on drawing him out. Students take out their notebooks and begin to write the day's learning intentions and start the warm-up. Miguel sits there silently, staring at his desk. He is hoping that he can make it through class with minimal interactions while going unnoticed.

Mrs. Howard circulates among the students, checking in with them while they get settled. As she comes around to Miguel, he avoids looking up or acknowledging her. She thinks to herself, *He has a lot of science to learn today, so I had better get him working*. She leans in and asks how he is, thinking, *I will show him I care by paying extra attention to him*. She thinks she knows why he is upset—he and his girlfriend must have had a fight. Miguel says nothing. He hopes that she will go away and stop asking questions. She places her hand on his shoulder and says: "Good morning, Miguel. How are you? Is everything okay?" She assumes that he likes the touch. It shows that she cares. Still no reply. Miguel feels uncomfortable with her touching him. He really wants to be left alone. She stands there, waiting and looking at him. She feels like he will come around, if she stays the course. She assumes he wants to connect with her.

After a minute of no response, she asks him to meet her in the hall so they can talk. She's thinking that he will open up if they talk one-on-one. *Surely*, she thinks, *he will share what's on his mind. He likes me and wants to share*. In reality, Miguel is confused and thinks that he is in trouble. He begins to feel angry.

Mrs. Howard heads out the door and into the hall. Miguel reluctantly follows, staring at the floor while his peers look up from their work to assess the situation. He wishes that she would leave him alone.

Once outside the room, Mrs. Howard inquires: "Miguel, what is wrong today? You can tell me. Is it Alisa?" She feels proud that she knows him so well. "Nothing . . . no," he replies. His heart races. He begins to sweat. He thinks about how he can make her questioning stop. *Why would she bring up Alisa, anyway?* "Nothing, really!" he pleads. He reasons that if he repeats himself she will stop. "It sure seems like something. You can tell me," she answers. She wants him to know that she cares, and it's her job to know details about him; he can rely on her. "Nothing!" he replies with a raised voice and a red face. He is now very angry. He wishes she would back away. He steps back. "I am worried. Tell me, Miguel. I am concerned," she presses. She steps in. She thinks, *If I persist, he will finally be able to share. Moving closer to him will create connection. It will be good for him to share his emotions and get it off his chest*.

"No!" he shouts. He storms away, back into the classroom and into his seat, head hung low, avoiding eye contact with his peers. Left standing there, Mrs. Howard experiences confusion and anger. She wonders why he did not respond to her. She tells herself, *Miguel simply doesn't care about me or my class; otherwise, he would tell me what is making him so upset*.

She comes back into the classroom without looking at him and begins the lesson. He missed the day's warm-up and loses points. He can't focus and wishes the class were over.

From an outside view, it's easy to get the sense that Miguel might feel like a trapped animal in a corner fighting for its life. The tension is palpable. According to Mrs. Howard's perspective, she is only trying to help and is concerned about his distress. Because she fails to read the signals that he sends, she makes the situation worse by pressing him, thereby intensifying his dysregulation. Sadly, the very connection that Mrs. Howard attempts to establish breaks down, possibly without hope of repair. Additionally, Miguel is agitated and most likely will be disengaged in the day's learning, all the while losing credit for the first assignment. One interaction, two interpretations: How did this go so wrong? With her lack of role clarity and boundary awareness, compounded by limited awareness and self-reflection, Mrs. Howard unintentionally escalates a situation that results in a fractured relationship, as well as a negative student grade. What would you do in this situation? What might you do differently in the future?

How to Develop Helpful Limits

There are multiple opportunities for teachers to work with students individually and in small groups, such as one-on-one conferences, lab groups, and learning teams. In providing these instructional structures, teachers have multiple chances to lean in and instruct students on a more personal and targeted level. When planning for this type of effective instruction, consider setting physical and emotional boundaries.

Physical Limits

In the case above, Miguel was signaling, using his body and his words, that he needed his space. In primary grades, children are taught to respect one another's "space bubbles." To do so, adults teach children to be aware of their own and others' personal space in order to create a sense of safety and comfort. Students are also taught to advocate for their protection by telling whoever the trespasser might be to "get out." In turn, both adults and students are taught to respond accordingly by honoring the boundary-setter and, thereby, encouraging children to entitlement over their own bodies.

It is no different for adolescents. Mrs. Howard made two significant mistakes. First, she entered into Miguel's "space bubble" through her close proximity, ignoring the signals he was sending. On several occasions, he relayed that he was not interested, or able, to connect with her at that time. He was setting a boundary with his body language, behavior, and lack of communication, made evident by his distance, avoidance, abruptness, and red face. The more Mrs. Howard leaned in, the more his resistance grew. She could have let up, meanwhile watching and waiting for the frost to wear off. This requires a lot of patience.

Second, in her well-meaning effort to connect, Mrs. Howard breached Miguel's boundary by touching his shoulder without his consent. In lieu of pulling back, she pressed on, which resulted in a physical boundary violation. He had not given her permission to do so. There are many students who may not be comfortable with physical interaction of this sort. In fact, for students with ACEs in their background, seemingly harmless interactions of this nature can create fear, sadness, and discomfort. Further, maintaining appropriate physical boundaries protects young people from misconstruing the meaning of touch.

Emotional Limits

Miguel's behavior helped him create a safe space to try to manage his emotions that he might not have been able to name. Most likely, he didn't even know the reason for his moodiness that day—as often adolescents don't. To assume that he could or would want to share with a teacher what was happening for him emotionally is risky and inappropriate. He is entitled to his own privacy. Positional authority does not give adults the right to have access to students' private lives. It is a common trap for well-intentioned teachers, like Mrs. Howard, to unwittingly press students around the distress they witness, then to find that they are ill-prepared to handle what students share or how they react. Knowing intimate details of students' lives does not make for a better teacher. The precarious nature of a boundary breach leaves both the teacher and the student exposed, and it often results in an unhealthy relationship—or no relationship at all. Other critical consequences can be student disengagement, failing grades, and absenteeism.

Part of caring for students is remembering the fact that they have personal boundaries that dictate how you should interact with them. They view you as an advocate and someone who has their best interests at heart. They rely on you to tell the truth, to be an adult, and to protect them. You want them to build solid boundaries so that they may navigate relationships with a keen awareness of what healthy boundaries look and feel like, regardless of their past experiences. Teachers have the opportunity to continually model healthy adult-child relationships, thus forging a template for safety, privacy, and comfort in their lives moving forward, all the while experiencing care and connection.

Figure 5.4 can help you think about boundaries within various relationship settings. It illustrates several types of boundaries and offers reflection questions for your consideration.

Figure 5.4 Boundary Types and Reflection Questions

Boundary Type	Relationship 1:1 student	Classroom 1: whole group
Emotional Feelings, reactions, moods, thoughts	Am I calm and safe? Am I managing my side of the fence?	Am I calm and safe? Am I acting as an adult professional?
Physical Skin, body, personal space	Am I touching others without permission? Am I aware of my own physical needs?	Do I touch my students? Am I aware of my own physicality?
Spatial Personal space, geographical	Am I respecting my and others' need for personal space? Am I "close talking"?	How is my room arranged? Is my room too cluttered or too barren?
Time Being on time, respecting and enforcing time limits	Do I show up on time? Do I respect other people's time?	Am I starting and ending class on time? Am I providing student feedback in a timely manner?
Language Inclusive vs. exclusive, appropriate for role	Can I say "no"? Am I being clear? Am I using my voice appropriately?	Am I communicating well? Are my words congruent with my role?
Ideals/Values Belief systems, cultural influence	Am I honoring, expressing, and acting from my values and beliefs?	Is my expression of my beliefs/values appropriate in my role?

The boundary types listed in Figure 5.4 shift and change in different environments and roles. Many educators have multiple roles—for example, administrator, coach, advisor, and club leader. How do you imagine a change in role impacts teacher-student boundaries? Just because boundaries or expectations might be more flexible or "loose" in one arena doesn't mean there are no limits at all, so how might you communicate the shift clearly to students whom you supervise in dual roles?

Role Clarity: What You Are and What You Are Not

As mentioned, teachers play many roles within a school community. The roles are not always clear, and that's why it's important to seek clarification, particularly in an effort to build and maintain healthy relationships. Caring for students is at the heart of education. Boundaries help keep adults and students on their own sides of the fence and prevent injury and broken relationships due to misunderstanding, a breach of trust, or unmet expectations. Figure 5.5 offers an Awareness Reflection Exercise to help you further define your interactions with students. Give yourself an opportunity to flesh out your responsibilities within the various roles you play. Clarity is essential—not only for you, but for your students also.

Figure 5.5   Awareness Reflection Exercise

As you consider your educator role and upholding boundaries, take a moment to reflect on the following aspects of the job.
Imagine that you are sharing this with your students.

- As your teacher, I am ____.

  As your teacher, I am not ____.

- As your coach, I am ____.

  As your coach, I am not ____.

- As your club sponsor, I am _______________________________________.

  As your club sponsor, I am not ____________________________________.

What is difficult for me in establishing and upholding boundaries in my many roles?

____

____

____

____

How might I need to redefine what it means for me to care for my students?

____

____

____

What do I feel like I might lose by establishing boundaries?

____

____

____

What questions do I have about how to clearly define my role within student relationships?

____

____

____

____

Fostering Wellness Through Curriculum and Instruction

There is a lot to learn in this world. There is a lot to teach, as well. Every year, there are more curricular and instructional materials available in the form of websites, apps, books, videos, simulations, projects, and labs. It's an exciting time for educators; there is more opportunity than ever right at your fingertips to curate and provide meaningful learning opportunities. With this opportunity comes a need for increased vigilance as you take into account the mental health needs of students who receive both the joy and stress of unrelenting information and resources. Your job as a teacher becomes, among other things, helping students navigate the literacy stampede (Gallagher, 2006). What might this look like in the classroom in terms of what you ask students to read and write? How do you help them survive the onslaught of information?

Mr. Cooper is a caring English teacher who is highly regarded by both his students and his peers. For years, he has been a student favorite because he works hard to make his courses interesting, rigorous, and fun. Students continually report back that they learn a lot in his classes. He connects well with students both in the classroom and on the field, where he is also a beloved soccer coach.

As part of his ongoing quest to select relevant and interesting texts for book clubs, Mr. Cooper provides five titles that he believes will offer a variety of choices for students. He plans to give time in class for students to "interview" each book, then list their top three selections, which he will review before assigning groups.

During the book interviewing process, there seems to be a lot of excitement about the options. Mr. Cooper speaks clearly about the topics of each book, and he asks students to make selections that interest them—that they are sure will capture their attention for the duration of the book club. He is pleased by the response, as he has spent significant time picking a list that takes into account student interest and includes fiction; nonfiction; topics of interest to boys, girls, and adolescents; and current topics. He reviewed websites and blogs pertaining to young adult readers, in addition to asking around as to what students might want to read.

By the end of the week, Mr. Cooper places each student in a book club of his or her choice, and the assignment is underway. Within two weeks, each group reads two to three chapters to prepare for the book club discussion.

All seems to be going well until Lexi fails to show up to the third discussion, then the fourth, and eventually misses several additional days of class.

Mr. Cooper worries, because Lexi is an excellent student. She is always prepared, contributes to whole- and small-group discussions, and is well liked by her peers. What could be going on?

Weeks later, with permission from Lexi and her family, the school counselor shares with Mr. Cooper that Lexi's parents report that she has been crying regularly and feels deeply sad. Lexi told the counselor that she could not stop thinking about her cousin who committed suicide last year at age 18. She explained that the book she was reading in book club brought her back to the reasons why her cousin might have killed himself and the times she may have been insensitive to his cries for help. She blames herself for not being more aware. She believes it was her fault, and she shares the guilt, like several people in the book.

Mr. Cooper never imagined that Lexi might be in this situation. He had no idea of the personal struggle that she was facing. As a caring and effective teacher, he was working to pull students into their learning by engaging them in high-interest topics and texts. He is devastated.

In debriefing with his assistant principal, Mr. Cooper relates that he would never intentionally place Lexi in harm's way or intentionally trigger her past trauma. He describes how he thoughtfully selects engaging text materials, accompanied by learning activities. He adds that, going forward, he will consider the impact that such choices may have on students' mental health. Because he values students' interests and their choices, he admits to his wish to not exclude books on topics that might be difficult or controversial, but he proposes that, next time, he take the added step of addressing the whole class verbally, and in the written directions, about the need for each of them to take into consideration their choices in light of fostering mental wellness. Having them ask themselves, *Is this a healthy choice for me to spend time on and give attention to?* could increase students' awareness about their own individual circumstances. This is an important move that focuses on stating clearly for students that some curricular materials may impact them in ways that they need to monitor.

In the following scenario, the teacher is utilizing what she knows about student trauma and chronic stress to redirect a writing assessment. Can you picture yourself in a similar situation? What might you do?

Ms. Fuentes uses journals to assess student understanding of various topics in the humanities. She frequently asks students to reflect on current events as a means of drawing a personal connection between what's happening in the world and what students are experiencing. It has been enlightening to note the various ways in which students connect to the world around them.

For Jorge, this week's journal entry is proving difficult, because the topic—immigration—strikes close to home. His mother was deported three months ago, leaving him, his three younger brothers, and his dad behind. Reading about separated families has drawn him into the reading, and motivates him to write, although he is so overcome with emotion that he cannot help silently sobbing every time he begins to write.

Ms. Fuentes knows Jorge well. She detects that he is unsettled and dysregulated. While assessing the article and his haphazard log entry, she infers the reason behind his distress. She gently says to him, "Jorge, while this article may be of interest to you, I would like you to step back and, in doing so, take care of yourself. It may be too difficult at this moment to put your thoughts into words. I do not want you to fight through it. I would like you instead to identify another article that you connect with, one that will not create so much stress. It's okay to do this. Let's touch base after class."

After class, Ms. Fuentes checks in to see how Jorge is. He is indeed calmer and has chosen to write a response to an article about self-driving cars, another topic that interests him. Ms. Fuentes also says that she notices that he might be carrying a lot of stress, and she affirms him for taking care of himself. She asks whether she can check in with him over the next couple of days about the assignment.

Ms. Fuentes is an astute teacher who is cognizant that for many students there will be topics, people, and events that will influence their wellness. For some, these will trigger profound stress and/or trauma. She is prepared to modify and adjust her expectations according to student input and, as in this case, observable student reaction. She is keenly aware that she is not a counselor, and she isn't comfortable acting as one. Furthermore, she maintains a vigilant mindset that alerts her to the possible impact on students' well-being of the activities she asks them to do and the topics she asks them to think about. As a teacher with knowledge of the importance of mental health, she helps Jorge make a better choice for himself.

As mentioned earlier, taking into account the roughly 44% of students who have experienced ACEs (CDC, 1997) can help them avoid connection to, or triggering of, trauma and stress. Acknowledging that so many students have suffered or are suffering events that heavily impact their development and learning, we can take extra steps to guide them in making curricular choices that are in the interest of their mental health. This is not censoring. This is being intentional in a way that incorporates who students are (whether we know their specific histories or not) and directs them toward healthy choices in what they learn and how they learn it.

Consider, also, that students (and most adults) experience various degrees of stress resulting from school safety issues, teen suicide, drug and alcohol use, competition, social pressure, and self-doubt. Given this reality, it's important to examine what students spend time on and think about. You have opportunities to elevate students and provide hope through the choices you help them make.

Unit and Lesson Planning With Healthy Relationships in Mind

Teacher-student relationships are at the center of effective teaching and learning environments. Pursuing healthy relationships requires forethought and planning. Figure 5.6 provides you with factors to consider in planning curriculum, instruction, and assessment that contributes to healthy relationships while helping students make choices for their well-being.

Taking Healthy Relationships School-Wide

Leaders set the pace in prioritizing healthy relationships and mental health. In Chapter 3, we discussed the importance of school leaders leading by example—in part by modeling self-care, and in part by upholding norms for behavior within the school community.

Figure 5.6   Healthy Relationships: Factors to Prompt Planning Decisions in Curriculum, Instructional Delivery, and Assessment

	The Factors				
	Boundaries (Physical, Emotional, Spatial, Time, Language, Ideals/Values)	Student Interests in Light of ACEs	Adolescent Developmental Appropriateness	Diversity, Equity, and Inclusion	School/District Identity and Values
Curriculum	Topics: Texts:	Topics: Texts:	Topics: Texts:	Topics: Texts:	Topics: Texts:
Instructional Delivery (Learning Activities)	Interactions between teacher and students: Interactions between students:	Interactions between teacher and students: Interactions between students:	Interactions between teacher and students: Interactions between students:	Interactions between teacher and students: Interactions between students:	Interactions between teacher and students: Interactions between students:
Assessment (Evidence of Student Learning)	Formative: Summative:	Formative: Summative:	Formative: Summative:	Formative: Summative:	Formative: Summative:

Healthy relationships are the product of healthy people. Healthy school cultures are the product of healthy people making the most informed decisions possible in order to foster safety and wellness. In order to make this goal a reality, leaders should consider providing mental health services to students and adults, assisting teachers in clarifying their roles, and establishing guidelines for interactions.

Mental Health Services

Students come to school carrying burdens; while most are able to bear them, others are not. Educators are astutely aware of students whose needs appear to outweigh school resources. Teachers talk over the coffeemaker and in the parking lot about students whose erratic behavior shows up as either overt behavior problems or nearly complete withdrawal. For each student who gets noticed for being at one of the two ends of this spectrum, many more act out or withdraw to a lesser degree.

Hearing students chant "mental health," "mental health" over and over during a press conference following a school shooting in Colorado brought home for us that students know what is needed to bring a sense of safety and stability. It seems obvious that, for all the interventions made available to best serve students, access to mental health services (ideally school-based) should be a high priority. Growing up is hard to do, especially in times as complicated as these.

Helping Teachers Know What the Job Is and What It Is Not

The role of teacher can be a difficult one to clearly define. Brooke remembers a student named Kenny, whose family background was riddled with extreme loss as well as inspiring resilience. He was a young man fighting to make a way through a tough upbringing and into a brighter future through education. It was easy to admire this student. Although he hardly ever smiled, he was a warm and kind person inside. As committed to making a future for himself as he was, Brooke, as his teacher, was equally committed to supporting him in whatever way possible. The question was not whether to care about him; it was about to what degree caring was appropriate in her role. So when she found herself driving Kenny and his girlfriend to the E.R. at midnight, she was clearly out of her role as a teacher.

Like most teachers, she had not received training on boundaries or guidance as to how to navigate tricky situations—such as giving rides to students; communicating via phone or text with students; offering money, food, or shelter to students; or taking on guardian-like roles for students. There are times when it may appear as if a student will not be okay if the teacher doesn't act in ways that could be deemed inappropriate or risky; teachers must not be left to make serious, life-impacting decisions on their own. Without clear guidance, teachers assume great emotional and physical responsibility. Despite good intentions, Brooke may have unknowingly put herself and Kenny at increased risk. It was by a stroke of luck that in this instance the situation was resolved without further incident.

Leaders must provide clear directions, protocols, and resources around the handling of students in crisis. Having a plan is critical, because if teachers know students well, care for them, and are interested in their well-being, sooner or later students' needs will surface. Therefore, supporting teachers in making decisions that protect them and serve students' best interests is at the heart of leadership.

Encouraging Clarity in Relationships

As the old adage states, "A chain is only as strong as the weakest link." A school community is only as strong as its ability to support everyone in it—every last one. Given the relationship-focused nature of schools, and the close quarters that adults and students share, awareness of boundaries is critical. Beyond awareness and clarity of roles, leadership can support teachers in promoting mutual agreements and provide accountability. Examples of this are ensuring that adults meet with students where there is "line of sight" and avoiding favoritism.

Recently, a teacher we know wondered whether it was okay to "friend" a student on social media. The student had found the teacher online and was hoping to connect in this way. The teacher felt uncomfortable with the request, because she had a lot of pictures of her personal life on her account, but she didn't want to risk being viewed as unfriendly. In the end, she made the correct choice and declined the friend request. Teachers are not friends; they are teachers—adults in charge of student learning and well-being. A school policy clarifying expectations for social-media use would have helped both her and her student navigate the situation more easily. Instead, she had to go it alone and, eventually, explain to the student her reasoning, which was brave and ultimately helpful in maintaining a healthy relationship.

Effective school leaders support teachers in establishing healthy boundaries and providing proper accountability. Role-playing, case studies, and consultation with mental health personnel assist teachers in building awareness and skills. Often, leaders who maintain a comprehensive viewpoint can provide guidance around policies related to student supervision, social-media policies, mandatory reporting laws, student safety, and adult safety. School administration can, and should, seek input from mental health professionals—either school-, district-, or community-based—in identifying policies that place healthy boundaries within a school culture. Clarity in relationships helps schools function effectively.

Reflections

Establishing and maintaining healthy boundaries is foundational to teaching and learning within school communities. Take a moment to reflect on your roles, relationships, and boundaries.

1. What impact does knowing about adverse childhood experiences (ACEs) have on my teaching, particularly related to physical and emotional boundaries?

2. Where do private and personal lives intersect?

3. What do I see as my role(s) as a teacher, coach, chaperone, director?

4. What might need to change for me in my role(s)?

____

____

____

5. What do I need from school leadership in order to do my job more effectively in this area?

____

____

____

____

Toolkit for Tomorrow

In an effort to cultivate healthy relationships, tomorrow I can:

- ❏ be aware of how ACEs show up in my classroom.
- ❏ be aware of my interactions with and impact on students with ACEs.
- ❏ examine where I might need to set clear boundaries.
- ❏ be intentional about setting and communicating those boundaries.
- ❏ plan curriculum, instruction, and assessment using lenses that build healthy relationships.
- ❏ seek support from mental health professionals in my school or district.
- ❏ ask for input from colleagues in maintaining healthy teacher-student relationships.
- ❏ trust my gut—if something doesn't feel right, then I will get support.
- ❏ partner with administration.
- ❏ lead with compassion . . . for myself and for others.

In the End, Be Loving

Having healthy boundaries means living with tensions:

- Being flexible *and* directive

- Being firm *and* loving

- Being static *and* dynamic

- Leading with the head *and* the heart

Negotiating a balance between these tensions is a requirement for ensuring safety, cultivating great relationships, and fostering optimal conditions for student learning.

Conflict Resolution

What to Do When Things Fall Apart

CHAPTER

6

An eye for an eye will only make the whole world blind.
—Mahatma Gandhi

"Mr. Brown hates me!" John, a high school junior, yells as he sits in the dean's office. He shakes his leg in an unconscious effort to diffuse the anger and anxiety in his body. John continues to stare at the invisible spot on the carpet, as tears well up and he blinks to hold them back. "I wasn't doing anything. He just hates me. He never helps me, and he is always yelling at me in front of everyone!" The dean sits quietly, allowing John to release his emotions until he is calm enough to engage. "I hate physics anyway," continues John. "Mr. Brown is a terrible teacher, and I don't care if I fail, because it's stupid anyway and I am never going to use it." This is the second time in a week that Mr. Brown has sent John to the dean with a detention for being disrespectful. In the first incident, two days ago, John repeatedly talked back after Mr. Brown corrected John's behavior. After processing helpful strategies with the dean, John apologized to Mr. Brown the next day. However, this morning, when John answered a question posed to the class, Mr. Brown responded with what John perceived as a sarcastic tone—another conflict ensued, and the relationship is broken. Without some kind of restorative process, the wounds on both sides will surely fester.

Conflict Resolution: Why Is It Important?

Conflict is inevitable. It is normal. Schools are already thriving, vibrant, passionate ecosystems where discourse is encouraged and important as part of a learning process. Add a mix of personalities, differing conflict styles (usually based on what was modeled early in life), and various individual experiences of trust and safety, and you have an environment ripe with possibility for things to fall apart, for relationships to dissolve, for resentment to fester, and for trust to break. It's going to happen. The good news is that conflict, misunderstanding, rigorous debate, and even hurt feelings are also incredible opportunities for learning, growth, and healing. It all depends on your mindset, your intention, your skill, your courage, and your action.

Resolving conflict is hard. Avoiding conflict seems a much easier solution, in the short term. However, avoidance leads to resentment, it fosters passive aggression, and it breaks down trust. Imagine a school community as a gorgeous tapestry composed of various colors and textures, each one contributing to the richness and beauty, all woven tightly together to create a sensational piece of fabric. When there is conflict among community members, it creates a tear in the fabric. If left unattended or ignored, the rip will continue to fray and denigrate the integrity of the fabric as a whole. If mended—although the shapes and textures may be changed forever—the tapestry will be stronger than before. This metaphor represents the philosophy of a restorative model of conflict. Mending takes time and resources. De-escalating a conflict and postponing, then circling back to, a hard conversation is different from avoidance. However, the benefits are immeasurable, not only to the school community but to our larger world as kids learn to resolve conflicts, not easily, but peacefully and effectively.

As highlighted in previous chapters, students with ACEs require safety and trust as foundations for learning. Safety and trust are lost when students or staff feel marginalized, disrespected, and, like John in the example above, "out" of relationship with no way to get a kid back "in." Pushing, kicking, or ignoring a child *out* of community is never a way *in*. Based on what we know about power dynamics, ACEs, and adolescent development, John had no choice but to give up and carry the anger and resentment and live outside of the community within Mr. Brown's classroom. Why is it worth the time and training to resolve conflict appropriately? Figure 6.1 lists some of benefits facing conflict rather than avoiding it.

Figure 6.1   Benefits of Facing and Resolving Conflicts

People are empowered	Misunderstandings get cleared up	Reduction in violence
Relationships are healthy and authentic	Increased confidence in one's ability to resolve conflict	Reduction in acting out or passive-aggressive behaviors
Trust exists	Messes get cleaned up	Positive culture shift
Accountability actually feels good	Safety	Increased sense of ownership in the community
Improved attendance (meetings, school, sports)	Conflict-resolution skills can prevent conflict	Reduction in detentions and other punishments

Student Experience

Adolescents are justice-oriented. It is part of their developmental process of figuring out who they are in relationship to others. They love to fight for a cause and are passionate about fairness. When they perceive they are being treated unfairly, their emotions intensify, and so can their behavior. Students want to feel heard and seen. They have strong beliefs, frequently rooted in black and white (i.e., all or nothing) thinking (this is connected to brain development and cognition, which we talked about in Chapter 1). Add boundary-pushing to the mix, and you have the perfect recipe for conflict.

In the example above, John has a strong reaction to Mr. Brown, which *may or may not* have anything to do with Mr. Brown. When looking through a lens of trauma and chronic stress, certain questions arise about John's reaction to Mr. Brown. Figure 6.2 offers some possibilities for underlying causes of John's behavior and reaction to the perceived conflict. Underneath anger, there is almost always pain of some kind. Looking through this lens allows you to be compassionate rather than reactive.

Figure 6.2 What Could Be Going on With John?

- John feels angry.
- John feels powerless.
- John feels as though he isn't liked.
- John feels frustrated.
- John feels singled out.
- John feels criticized.
- John feels like he can't do anything right.
- John feels defensive.
- John may be reacting to Mr. Brown based on a family history of "being yelled at."

Maybe Mr. Brown behaved in a way that warranted John's intense reaction, and maybe he didn't. Because the dean was able to let John express his feelings, while listening deeply to hear what was happening below the content, John had an opportunity to calm down, regroup, and look at the situation differently. This step is a necessary prerequisite to problem-solving. As we discussed in Chapter 2, adolescents can't problem-solve when their nervous system is dysregulated. Taking time to let John express his emotions and then settle enabled John to see his part in the conflict without solely laying blame on Mr. Brown (as evidenced by John's willingness to apologize after the first incident). If Mr. Brown were able to listen deeply to John's concerns, he might wonder about John's life experience with conflict, feeling criticized, powerlessness, and defensiveness. This would help Mr. Brown not take things personally, stay in his appropriate adult role, and not get sucked into or provoke conflict with John. Mr. Brown wouldn't be personally offended that John doesn't know how to do a physics problem, nor should he be offended that John doesn't (yet) know how to resolve a conflict appropriately, until someone teaches him.

Adult Experience

Think for a moment about how conflict was or wasn't managed in the family you grew up in. How has that influenced the way you deal or don't with conflict when it shows up in your life? Adults may have more experience dealing with or avoiding conflict based on their life history, yet unless clear communication and processes for resolving conflicts are in place, the result is often that relationships, safety, and trust are compromised. People who have experienced chronic stress and trauma most likely have little or no experience resolving conflict appropriately. They have not had skills modeled to them, and based on the kinds of ACEs they lived through, it is reasonable to assume they have been witness to high-conflict situations in their home, as many ACEs naturally are associated with conflict. Resolving conflict can feel really uncomfortable, intimidating, and scary. Figure 6.3 highlights some reasons why people avoid conflict altogether.

Figure 6.3   Reasons People Avoid Conflict

• Power imbalances exist	• Fear of consequences
• Fear of losing control	• Lack of trust in the process or other person involved
• Fear of looking foolish or weak	• Past experience that went wrong
• Resolving conflict is hard and uncomfortable	• Vulnerability is scary
• Fear of being in trouble	• Inexperience
• Needing to save face	• Culture doesn't support a restorative model
• Fear of being hurt	• Fear of retribution or retaliation ("snitches get stitches")

Foundation for Effective Practice #1: Punishment Doesn't Work

At some level, you already know this. If punishment *did* work, you would never write more than one detention slip at the beginning of the year. That first detention slip would stop a student's bad behavior or poor choice, scare the rest of the class into submission by having them witness what happens to "troublemakers," and teach all kids a lesson about expectations and good behavior. That's all it should take: one detention slip. In reality, what that detention slip does is send a message to the student who is dysregulated, upset, insecure, angry, or unable to do what you are asking that *he or she is a bad kid*. What motivation is there for students to change their behavior when they feel targeted, ashamed, helpless, and afraid? Research shows that fear (e.g., fear of punishment) inhibits learning. Fear consumes psychological resources, diverting them from parts of the brain that manage working memory and process new information.

As a result, how psychologically safe people feel strongly shapes their propensity to engage in learning behaviors, such as information sharing, asking for help, and experimenting (Edmondson, 2019). Not to mention that if they could do something different, they would. Students want to be "in" the fold, not "out." That is always what they want, even when they don't know how to do it well.

Foundation for Effective Practice #2: Ownership, Accountability, and Empathy Matter

When mistakes are made, feelings get hurt, misunderstandings occur, and anger erupts, there needs to be some system for repairing the damage. That repair may come in the form of a simple acknowledgment and ownership of your part of the conflict or an apology. Owning your part in a misunderstanding or conflict is the first step in resolving it. It is rare that only one person is solely responsible for conflicts. If you don't see your part initially, then get curious, take some time, and dig a little deeper.

Having empathy and the ability to look past your own feelings and reactions to imagine what the other person may be feeling is useful in moving toward win-win solutions to conflicts. Empathy is about connecting with the *emotion* that someone is experiencing, *not the event* or the circumstance (Brown, 2012). Taking time to empathize with a student in distress before problem-solving and moving into "fix-it" or "punish-it" mode will help the student feel seen by and connected with you. Let's say a student comes in complaining about how tired he or she is. Rather than react by saying something like "You should get an alarm clock," or "I know what you mean; I am tired too," you might instead respond with "I see how tired you are, and I can imagine what it took for you to get here this morning. I am glad you are here" before moving on to "What feels possible this morning?" It will also help the student calm down, regulate, and reengage his or her brain before moving into next steps. What processes or protocols are in place at your school to allow students, when things blow up, to diffuse their intense emotions before engaging in problem-solving?

Foundation for Effective Practice #3: Clear Communication Is the Ticket

Clarifying, reframing, question-asking, and active listening are all communication skills needed to prevent or resolve conflict. They are the same skills needed to make a repair, so that there can be resolution and not re-traumatization. Teaching, practicing, and learning basic communication skills is key to being able to resolve conflict, especially when students (and many adults) have little to no experience using words to resolve conflicts appropriately.

Asking clarifying questions or using statements like the following can work wonders, because they reduce opposition by establishing the search for common ground:

- "Help me understand where you are coming from."
- "I don't quite understand yet; tell me more."
- "I am curious about . . ."
- "I'd love to know more about your perspective."
- "Just to clarify, here is where I was coming from . . ."
- "I think we may have had a misunderstanding; here is what I am wondering . . ."

Foundation for Effective Practice #4: Assume Good Intentions

Intentions and positive regard matter. When in conflict, we often presume the worst in the other person's actions or intentions. Good communication happens when the message the sender intended is the message understood by the recipient. When that doesn't happen, conflict ensues. The next time someone says or does something that offends you, try stepping back, taking a breath, and imagining the other person may not have intended to upset or harm you. Are there other possibilities? Could it be that this person was lacking communication skills, being reactive, or feeling defensive and hurt?

Foundation for Effective Practice #5: Preparation Is Key

Practicing preparation for conflict is important so that when it erupts, you have strategies at your disposal for de-escalating it. There is typically a tipping point, a moment even, when things escalate. Although it can happen fast, it usually doesn't come out of nowhere (even when it feels like it does). Here are some hints to help you recognize when things are about to fall apart and suggestions of how to de-escalate in those moments when the conflict is unpreventable or you did not attend to the warning signs in time. Heightening awareness of your own internal process and observing your students closely will help you recognize, prevent, or attend to conflicts as they happen. First, however, you may need to adjust your mindset around conflict. Understand that conflict is *going to happen*. Conflict doesn't have to be destructive; it can be trust-building and *beneficial to personal growth*. You *can handle difficult emotions* associated with conflict. It's uncomfortable, but you *can* do it.

Warning Signs:

- Body language (increased energy, movement, flushed face, changes in breathing, eye contact, dysregulated nervous system)

- Change in tone or voice (yelling, snapping, loud voice, angry, sarcastic, or silent)

- Spike or drop-off in emotion (increased frustration, anger, crying)

- Change in behavior (withdrawn, aggressive, passive aggressive, defiance)

Tips for De-Escalating Conflict:

- *Stay calm* and *observe*, without getting hooked into the content (what the conflict seems to be about). Manage your body, reactions, voice, and tone. Breathe. Slow down. Take a break. Creating space and hitting the "pause" button allows for things to calm and settle.

- *Drop the rope.* When you find yourself in a metaphoric or energetic tug-of-war with a student (or colleague), imagine dropping the rope. You will feel the relief of surrendering the struggle and can make better choices (actually listen to the other person) when you are not focused on winning.

- *Choose your battles.* It's okay to sacrifice a short-term "win" (e.g., saving face or being right) for the long-term one (improving the relationship by working through conflict when things calm down). De-escalating in the moment in favor of the true "win" is a more effective choice.

- *Disengage* as soon as you realize you are triggered. Once you notice things are escalating, it's okay to say something like "Hey, (student's name), I think we are both frustrated. How about we take some time to calm down, and we can talk later. I know we can figure this out, together. Why don't you take five minutes to get a drink or use the restroom, and come back as soon as you feel ready." Welcome the student back warmly.

- *Clarify.* Say what you mean. *Listen deeply.* Ask clarifying questions to understand the other person's experience, before misunderstandings take on a life of their own.

- *Don't take it personally*, and be loving. When you know you are triggered, check your ego. Approach the situation with *compassion*—first for yourself, and then for the other person.

Remember, when a person's nervous system is activated, he or she is not able to listen, learn, or think clearly. Taking time to de-escalate and calm down will be your best hope to make it through challenging situations.

What Works in the Classroom: Accommodating Conflict

As discussed earlier, conflict is unavoidable, and most people intrinsically avoid it. In a classroom environment, it is helpful to plan for *when* things will fall apart, not *if* they will. There are several ways for teachers to accommodate conflict within a classroom community: through making effective apologies, intentionaly framing classroom discipline (reengagement) systems, and designing curricular and instructional experiences around conflict.

Make Effective Apologies

Saying "my bad" is *not* an apology. There is an art to apologizing. True apology is a humbling act. A vulnerable act. A courageous act. Owning up to your mistakes—times when you have not been your best self or have been thoughtless, oblivious to someone else's feelings or experience, inconsiderate, or harmful—is paramount when it comes to building trust in a relationship of any kind. It is, somewhat sadly, a lost art. In a larger culture that seems to support punishment over reconciliation, blame over accountability, and conflict over peace, it is no wonder that students today have next to no experience with appropriate ways to resolve a conflict, much less apologize when it is appropriate to do so.

As an adult working with adolescents (and perhaps some adults) who have little or no experience apologizing, you have a tremendous opportunity to build trust if you are willing to apologize. Being vulnerable and owning your mistakes is a powerful tool for your educator arsenal. A high school math teacher recently came to us after a presentation and said, "I remember the first time I apologized to my students after being really cranky the day before, and they stared at me with their mouths gaping. Seriously, it was like they had never heard an adult apologize to them before. And it really shifted things in the classroom for the rest of the year, not only because the kids responded well, but I felt so much better after doing it."

In her book *Why Won't You Apologize?* Harriet Lerner talked about how an apology is a gift to the person harmed, and a gift to the relationship. Her third reason seems the least obvious and most powerful of reasons, and that is the gift that the apology offers to ourselves.

> The apology is also a gift to our self. Our self-respect and level of maturity rest squarely on our ability to see ourselves objectively, to take a clear-eyed look at the ways that our behavior affects others, and to acknowledge when we've acted at another person's expense. The good apology also earns us respect in the eyes of others, even though we may fear the opposite. (Lerner, 2017, pp. 175–176)

A basic apology contains the following ingredients:

- Willingness

- Honesty/sincerity

- Accountability

- Empathy

Mr. Brown catches John in the hallway after class. "Hey, John, may I speak with you for a moment?" Reluctantly, John replies, "Okay." Mr. Brown proceeds. "I am wondering if you are willing to talk with me for a few minutes? I would like to apologize for my comments to you earlier in the week." John looks at the ground. "It's okay, mister," he says. At this point, it would be easy to leave the matter there, but Mr. Brown knows it would be better not to and understands that he needs to be a role model for John. So he owns his part in the conflict and states what he wants for the relationship: "No, John, my behavior was not okay, and if it is okay with you, I would like to take a few minutes to clear the air, because you are an important member of my class, and I think it would be good for us to be able to move forward." "Okay," John says uncomfortably.

It is important to have awareness about John's reluctance. In this scenario, John is uncomfortable because he is not used to having an adult apologize to him. If John were experiencing intense emotions like he was in the dean's office, it would not be a good time for Mr. Brown to have this conversation with John, as he would need to cool down first. Mr. Brown is moving forward with his apology because he senses that John feels awkward but not unwilling.

Certainly, there are complex situations that require complex apologies; however, in the case of Mr. Brown and John, a basic apology will suffice. The purpose of Figure 6.4 is to help with language and increase awareness about the key parts that are the foundation of any apology. It lists some prompts and characteristics to be included in an apology from Mr. Brown to John.

Often, especially when working with teenagers, people believe that they will lose power and respect if they apologize or that their ownership or "admission of guilt" will be seen as weakness. Like most people, at some point in your life you have probably received an apology that lacked authenticity, was ignorant of the true offense, or was even more harmful to your feelings than the original event itself. If so, you are familiar with the yucky feelings and residual harm that comes with someone else's lack of personal awareness and accountability. Conversely, if you have ever received an appropriate apology, you know the healing power it has for

Figure 6.4 Ingredients for a Basic Apology

Prompts	Ingredient Checklist
"John, are you willing to take a few minutes to talk with me? I would like to apologize and clear the air."	Is the person ready and willing to hear your apology?
"You are an important member of our class, and I think we got off on the wrong foot. I would like things to be better between us."	Honesty and sincerity
"John, the other day I singled you out in class and was sarcastic and rude to you. I was frustrated and short-tempered, and I took it out on you."	Accountability and owning your mistakes
"I can imagine my words were upsetting and hurtful to you."	Empathetic response
"I am sorry for the way I treated you."	Say the words "I am sorry"
"In the future, I will be more mindful of the way I speak to you, and I hope you know that I enjoy having you in class and appreciate your contributions and participation. So, tomorrow, when you come back to class, it's a fresh start!"	Future hopes, expectations, and reentry plan

all parties involved. Hopefully, you recognize the power and influence you have when working with teenagers and that you take a risk to be vulnerable, when appropriate, and own what you need to in order for the fabric of your school to be stronger.

Foster a Culture That Focuses on Engagement and Reentry

Part of growing up is challenging rules and testing boundaries. Many students develop the skill to navigate the tension between their desire to push and knowing when to pull back just enough not to suffer consequences that jeopardize relationships. Some, especially those with little role-modeling and skill building, lack the know-how to manage this balance. This is where teachers come in to support students by reminding them of the effective steps to take when damage is done, in addition to providing support as they develop their skills. An apology is not necessarily required for reentry.

As discussed in Chapter 5, establishing clear expectations for both student and teacher behavior helps all members of the classroom community be successful. In John's case, it's important for him to know the expectations for Mr. Brown's class, including those that are related to managing inevitable conflict. Do students know what the rules and boundaries are? Is it clear as to the due process that results from infractions in the rules and breaches in boundaries? Has a reentry plan been discussed? Ideally, Mr. Brown has taken that time at the beginning of the school year to establish such clarity. Students make their best choices when they are informed.

As uncomfortable as it can be for adults to reenter relationships with other adults with whom they've been in conflict, imagine how hard it is for students.

Design Curriculum and Instruction That Deals With Conflict

Recently in a social-studies team planning meeting, the topic of respectful discourse came up—not unusual, given the current tumultuous political and social environment. Each teacher expressed the need to provide students ongoing opportunities to disagree with one another while displaying respect and offering one another dignity. The conversation centered on a common question: "If students don't learn these skills and practice them in school, where else will they have the opportunity?" There was a consensus that adults in the news weren't doing a great job of respectfully disagreeing with one another, so there was not a bevy of current role models the students could look to.

The teaching team set out to design a weekly current-events discussion, as one means of practice, which would provide students opportunities to read a news topic, share their thinking about the topic, and then discuss. There were several features to the structured discussions that fostered fairness and respect, starting with Norms for Classroom Discussion, as shown in Figure 6.5. Each teacher agreed to share and consistently uphold these Norms for Classroom Discussion. As a team, they were able to come back together and share ideas about what went well using this instructional model, along with how to refine it in order for students to best navigate difficult discussions.

Figure 6.5   Norms for Classroom Discussion

- Assume positive intentions.
- Listen intently to the speaker.
- Keep an open mind.
- Stick to the facts, not the feelings.
- Respect opposing views and the viewer.
- Agree to disagree.
- Each voice matters; everyone participates.

The conditions for meaningful discussion, and often disagreement, result from establishing norms. As students spend more time practicing conflict skills, as in weekly current-events discussions, have them take time to reflect on the degree to which their discussions do or do not reflect the agreed-upon norms. You will find that students are remarkably candid about whether their group, and whether they as individuals, uphold the norms. With ongoing practice, students will develop a self-awareness of and skill set in effective discourse.

Students need a structure for discussion that is potentially controversial in nature, particularly since many students don't come to school equipped with the knowledge and skill to healthily navigate controversy. There are a number of options available through curricular resources, yet such structure need not be complicated to implement. Figure 6.6 provides a straightforward protocol that prepares students for constructive engagement in a student-led current-events discussion.

Figure 6.6   Protocol for Classroom Discussion

Step 1—Selection: Students sign up to share a current event on a particular date. The date is far enough in advance to provide adequate time for students to select an article of interest from a reliable news source.

Step 2—Preparation: Each student checks in with the teacher about his or her event selection no later than a week prior to the discussion. Together they create a question or questions for the audience to consider, such as "What is your opinion about driverless cars? Why is this?"

Step 3—Discussion: (approx. 10–15 mins. per current event)

- Students gather in a circle in order to see one another. (Reading facial expressions and gestures is important to communication.) Students each have a copy of the article, which they read prior to the discussion.
- Students are reminded of the norms.
- Students are asked to keep their responses to approximately 1–2 minutes.
- The presenter shares the question and his or her response.
- Next, students are invited to share. (Not all students will have the opportunity to share, most likely.) The teacher keeps track of the discussion: who participates and what is said.
- The presenter summarizes what he or she has heard throughout the discussion and shares how his or her thinking and ideas have changed—or why they have not.
- The presenter thanks the participants, and they turn and thank one another.

Step 4—Debrief: Individually, students are asked to reflect on the process aspect of the discussion: What went well? What needs refinement? Then, as a group, they report out.

In addition to participating in civilized discussion about current events, the students in this example are asked to explore provocative questions that require them to seek answers through research. Take questions such as "Why does the United States have a drone program?" or "Who is most responsible for and vulnerable to the changing climate?" (The Choices Program, 2019). The students are pushed to consider serious problems and build solutions by reading articles from various sources, thus developing a point of view according to what they read. Then, they work in small groups to define various answers, which sometimes are oppositional; for example, "The use of drones in U.S. military operations will save military lives" versus "Use of drones will create more loss of foreign civilian life." The students are forced to recognize the complexity of problems and the reality that there are few simple solutions.

Classrooms can be places where students wrestle with ideas and challenge themselves to consider their opinions in light of values and facts. For many students who have never been asked their opinions, or required to develop one, such learning opportunities not only foster voice, but also develop cognitive skills such as understanding, determining what's important, and formulating questions. In addition, letting your students know they are free to change their minds or extend their understanding by learning from one another models adaptability, which they may not have seen elsewhere. Diana Hess, a leader in the use of controversy as a teaching tool, explains that "in a time that's so hyperpartisan and hyperpolarized, we want to model for students the importance of being willing to change one's mind. It's hard for someone to take a public position on something and then to change their mind" (Richardson, 2017). This type of flexibility helps students manage conflict by not getting stuck in one perspective or feeling as though they can't modify their point of view once it has been stated; they are free to change course.

Taking Conflict Resolution School-Wide

A restorative justice discipline model requires the creation and implementation of processes for students and staff to engage in meaningful conflict-resolution measures that honor the dignity of both the individual and the community. This approach takes time, training, and willingness. The benefits of focusing on accountability and repair, as opposed to punishment, are the foundation for school communities to become safe places of deep connection, where learning of all kinds can thrive.

Implement a Restorative Justice Model

If a restorative model is new for you and you are open to exploring it, know that it is going to feel uncomfortable for a while. You may feel like students are "getting one over on you," especially if you come from a traditional model that says they are "acting out on purpose" or "manipulating" you and therefore should be punished.

In Chapter 2, we proposed that all behavior is adaptive. As humans, we all adapt and "manipulate" situations for our survival. When you look at students' behavior through an adaptive lens, you can see that students aren't doing something to you so much as doing something for themselves—to survive. As an educator, consider accepting the challenge of helping students adapt in healthier and more effective ways.

Howard Zehr (2002) defined restorative justice as a lens composed of principles, values, and respect:

> Ultimately, however, the basic value that is supremely important is respect: respect for all, even those who are different from us, even those who seem to be our enemies. Respect reminds us of our interconnectedness but also of our differences. Respect insists that we balance concern for all parties. If we pursue justice as respect, we will do justice restoratively. (Zehr, p. 36)

Beliefs and values also inform how a school community addresses conflict.

> If conflict is seen through a belief system that recognizes students are not miniature adults, but developing people, we may presume their actions are intentional and that reprimands and punishment will result in change. Thinking about them as developing people we presume their actions indicate they are struggling to handle something difficult and they need support. The first perspective includes values such as obedience, perfection, compliance, and assimilation. The second includes values such as honesty, trust, encouragement, support, relationship and collaboration. (Evans & Vaandering, 2016)

What students with chronic stress and trauma need in a disciplinary system is an opportunity to calm down, reset, and get support if needed so that they can return to class, in an emotional state that is conducive to being an active, appropriate community member. It is a way of honoring them. Cutting students out of the fabric of community with no means of really learning (understanding the impact of their behavior on both themselves and others) and making a repair is ineffective, mean, and harmful to a developing child. Kids need to know they are loved, valued members of their community, even—and *especially when—they mess up.*

A restorative model *is not* about a lack of consequences; it *is* about capitalizing on a learning opportunity to be accountable for your actions, having an opportunity to make a repair if necessary, and being intentionally welcomed back into the fold of the fabric of community. When people have an opportunity to make things right and restore what was damaged, all parties are able to truly move forward with an increased sense of trust, possibility, growth, and real change. Figure 6.7 highlights some basic differences between a punitive model and a restorative one.

Figure 6.7   Distinctions Between Restorative and Punitive Models

Restorative Model	Punitive Model
Process-oriented (depthful—takes time)	Band-Aid: Quick fix
Relationship-focused (individual and collective)	System-focused
Restorative in its nature (values restitution)	Punitive in its nature (values punishment)
"Lessons" taught by assuming responsibility	"Lessons" taught by accepting punishment
People are defined by their capacity to grow and change—asset-based	People are defined by how they don't measure up—deficit-based

Be Willing to Have Hard Conversations

We have to be able to talk to each other when things are hard. To do that, it is necessary to be able to tolerate uncomfortable feelings in order to have difficult conversations. Know that you can make it through a hard conversation, and remember that the relationship is worth the discomfort. The authors of *Crucial Conversations* described these types of conversations as having three parts: opposing opinions, high stakes, and strong emotions (Patterson, Grenny, McMillan, & Switzler, 2012). Classrooms are places where all three of those ingredients naturally exist. Students and teachers are passionate and opinionated. The stakes are high, because unresolved conflict has the power to erode the development and sustainability of relationships, which jeopardizes student learning. When conflict occurs, hard conversations need to happen, and, for that, trust and safety must be present. If your school already has a culture of equity, where every type of thread and textile is seen and respected, and accountability is a shared value, then engaging in uncomfortable but necessary dialogue is a lot easier. For the rest of us, this is hard work.

Think of your school community. Are people able to have open, honest, and constructive conversations? Is there psychological safety in your community? Is it a place where people can be forthright and open when it comes to addressing an issue? Are there opportunities for professional learning to increase skills for students and adults alike? Do you know what shared agreements about resolving conflict would look like in your community? If the answer to these questions is "no," what small steps might you take to increase awareness about the need to learn more or build skill in this area?

Model Your Values

Leaders form school culture as well as bring it to life through actions and words. It is nearly impossible to parcel out belief from practice: The two are intertwined, since one informs the other. If a school leader values honest, harmonious, and heartfelt interactions, then he or she will lead by example in choosing to face conflict and the accompanying uncomfortable emotions. Conflict resolution and relationship-building cannot exist without trust. What are you doing as a school leader to build trust within relationships? Are you trustworthy? Does your walk match your talk? Shame researcher Brené Brown, in *Dare to Lead* (2018), pointed out that "when we are struggling with trust and don't have the tools or skills to talk about it directly with the person involved, it leads us to talk about people instead of to them" (p. 222). Imagine reframing conflict as an opportunity to cultivate relationships rather than as something to be avoided for fear of losing those relationships. Imagine, also, that other people have a shared desire to experience healthy relationships that are based on trust and, thus, want to learn to handle conflict more effectively. Essentially, upholding the notion that *we are all in this together* can be a helpful mindset in staying open to the possibility of conflict in our schools. In this instance and in many others, leadership affords many moments for others to see, hear, and notice the values that they hold within their hearts.

Reflections

Working through conflict is essential to healthy relationships. Take a few minutes to reflect on your own relationship to conflict and how it shows up in your classroom. Creating awareness and being prepared will help you the next time a conflict arises.

1. What do I know about my own conflict style?

2. What are some small ways I can start to appropriately address "little things that bug me" as a way to practice my conflict-resolution skills at work?

3. In what ways do my classroom policies and procedures antic-ipate the reality of conflict, along with constructive ways to resolve it?

4. Where can I get support to resolve a conflict, if I feel like I need someone to mediate or simply witness a crucial conversation?

Toolkit for Tomorrow

In an effort to resolve conflict, tomorrow I can:

- ❑ increase awareness around my own conflict style and reactivity.
- ❑ notice when I start to get triggered, so that I can de-escalate before engaging with a student or colleague.
- ❑ presume goodwill and positive regard of those I am in conflict with.
- ❑ create safety for the person I need to have a "crucial conversation" with.
- ❑ think creatively about discipline in my classroom to focus on the teacher-student relationship and keeping students "in" the fold.
- ❑ breathe and lead with my heart first.
- ❑ start to develop conflict-resolution skills by addressing the little things that I would prefer to ignore. It will help build my muscles for the big stuff.
- ❑ lead with compassion . . . for myself and for others.

In the End, Be Loving

Be the person you are meant to be. Don't let conflict ruin your relationships and impede opportunities to learn. Have courage and take a risk to deepen trust by addressing what you need to in a loving and direct way. You will feel better, and your relationships will thrive and be healthier. The more frequently that conflict gets resolved, the less it will seem to come up. Try it. You'll see.

Integrating It All

What's the world for if you can't make it up the way you want it?
—Violet, in Toni Morrison's *Jazz* (1992)

Danielle sighs as she sits in her seat by the window in her senior math class. She lays her head on her desk, waiting for the bell to ring as she takes out her binder. As she reaches in her backpack, she realizes that it is not there. *Crap.* In her angst, she realizes that today is the quiz. She knows that she wrote it down but forgot. She knows it's Thursday; however, given her cold and acute asthma early this week, she missed two days of school. Panicked, she tries to figure out what to do, although she is simply too tired to figure out a single next step.

In addition to not feeling well, she was up most of the night unable to sleep, although she was really tired. She ended up on her Instagram account for several hours to pass the time. In browsing posts by her friends, she discovered that she had not been invited to a party over the weekend. This makes her both sad and angry. *It must be because I am ugly and fat*, she thinks. *Who cares anyway? They're dumb!*

Simultaneously, she is trying to remember where she could have left her binder. She wonders whether she left it at her workplace. She decides that it has to be at her mom's house, which is the last place she remembers using it. She has been at her dad's since the weekend, so she figures that the binder must be on her mom's kitchen table, where she left it Saturday. Funny that her mom didn't call, but then she realizes that she has been out of town working. With her thoughts swirling and her exhaustion looming, she sits limply. Her classmates take their seats next to her. Her friend Marty notices that Danielle is looking off, so he asks her, "Are you okay?" She shrugs in response while looking blankly at her desk.

The teacher, Ms. Samson, takes note that Danielle is back at school, so she makes a point of checking in and saying hi during the warm-up activity. As she does, she notices Danielle's hunched shoulders, her sad expression, and the dark circles under her eyes. She gently tells her that she is glad to see her back and asks how she is feeling, knowing that she was out sick (a fact that Marty had shared with her earlier that week). Danielle looks up wearily at Ms. Samson, who smiles warmly. It's obvious to Ms. Samson that she is in distress—why and to what degree she does not know; however, she intends to pay particular

(Continued)

(Continued)

attention during the class period in order to determine what next steps are necessary to support Danielle, who is generally not a student who shows her struggles externally.

The class period proceeds from the warm-up to the quiz. Danielle musters the energy to complete as much of the five-question assessment as possible. She wants to cry. Ms. Samson notices this, in addition to the quiz that is barely filled out. This is not usual for Danielle. She is a strong math student. While the remainder of the students are completing the quiz, Ms. Samson gently asks Danielle if she wants to grab a drink or move around for the next five minutes or so. Danielle nods her head yes and silently leaves, returning when the rest of the students have completed the quiz.

Following the assessment, Danielle joins her small group that includes three other students with whom she has been working for the past four weeks. She is relieved to see them, because she won't have to participate with the whole class. That just seems like a lot today. She knows that, for the remainder of the class, she will be working with her small group, and this makes her feel like she has the energy to connect. The four of them engage in the learning task by settling into their collaborative roles. She likes the fact that they work together to complete the problem-based math task, record the solution, discuss their reasoning, and clean up the materials. She focuses on the math. She feels good about her contribution. She has a moment when she feels successful.

During class, Ms. Samson circulates among each group. She observes and listens in. When a moment to target instruction presents itself, she provides information to help the group move forward with the problem. In Danielle's group, Ms. Samson watches as they persist in each step of the problem. She is pleased to see Danielle appear more relaxed, while contributing her thinking to the process. She kindly asks Danielle to stay after class for a few moments so that they can touch base.

After class, Ms. Samson explains that she noticed that Danielle doesn't seem like her usual self. She inquires after Danielle's well-being: "I notice that you seem worn out. Is there anything I can do to support you?" Danielle shares briefly the source of her stress and tiredness, including some personal details about her parents' divorce, her illness, the demand to perform at school, and her job. Ms. Samson empathizes with her feelings of stress and being overwhelmed while not pressing for more detail. Ms. Samson takes the opportunity to remind Danielle of several facts: (1) She is a valuable member of the learning community and is missed when she is gone; (2) she has options like utilizing the revision policy for the quiz, to meet Ms. Samson after school for tutoring, and to utilize their Google Classroom to get caught up; and (3) she has available to her a network of people who support her: her teachers, her family, her friends, and the school counselor. Finally, Ms. Samson encourages Danielle to take care of herself by being attentive to her health and her needs. She asks that Danielle check in with her later in the day or tomorrow and let her know how she is doing and whether she has accessed her resources. Danielle agrees and feels relieved to have a teacher who cares about her both as a student and as a person.

Integrating Practices in Teaching, Learning, and Mental Health: Why Is It Important?

This chapter and the story of Danielle and Ms. Samson illustrate what is possible. It's not enough to focus only on the foundational practices associated with curriculum design, instructional delivery, and assessment. Knowing what plays out for students, and adults, in the social and emotional aspects of school directs practitioners to incorporate effective practices in mental health into the commonly held role of the teacher—particularly in secondary schools, and specifically with students experiencing trauma and chronic stress. To look only at the fundamentals of teaching and learning without thoughtful examination and integration of psychosocial sciences leaves teachers at a disadvantage in their ability to serve the whole student. Offering an integrated approach to education provides a pathway through chaotic situations into those which are more stable.

Student Experience

Danielle shows up to class because she is aware that attending school is in line with her goals. Her high school cultivates a "college-going culture." When she was a freshman, her advisor talked with her about the purpose of high school according to what Danielle might want out of life. Danielle can articulate that graduating from high school is important to her. She wants to go on to college. She believes that postsecondary options will help her get a good job and offer her options for employment and lifestyle not available to her parents, whom she has witnessed work diligently throughout their lives. She wants opportunity.

Adult Experience

From the outside, Danielle looks downtrodden. She has been absent due to illness. She performs poorly on her schoolwork. Knowing the specific reasons behind these events is not what is important; rather, inferring the struggle that she is experiencing is what helps her teacher make decisions to both preempt and to respond, regardless of why Danielle might be distressed. In fact, often it's difficult to really know what lies beneath students' behavior in the classroom. Danielle is entitled to her privacy, so one can only infer the cause behind her actions if left unexpressed. What Ms. Samson does know is that she will need to rely on the practices she already uses, such as consistent routines and kindness, and engage in some additional ones, such as partnering with colleagues.

What Works in the Classroom: Teaching and Learning With Trauma in Mind

Ms. Samson is a skilled and compassionate teacher. She knows a lot about the elements of effective teaching and learning: classroom culture, curriculum design, instruction, and assessment. She also knows that she can't fix all that is wrong with her students' life experiences. Therefore, she operates out of her locus of control, making decisions that positively impact her students and leaving behind those that don't. Ms. Samson combines effective practices in teaching and learning with practices in mental health, resulting in an integrated model that mitigates the effects of chronic stress and trauma.

Figure 7.1   Five Lenses for Teaching, Learning, and Mental Health

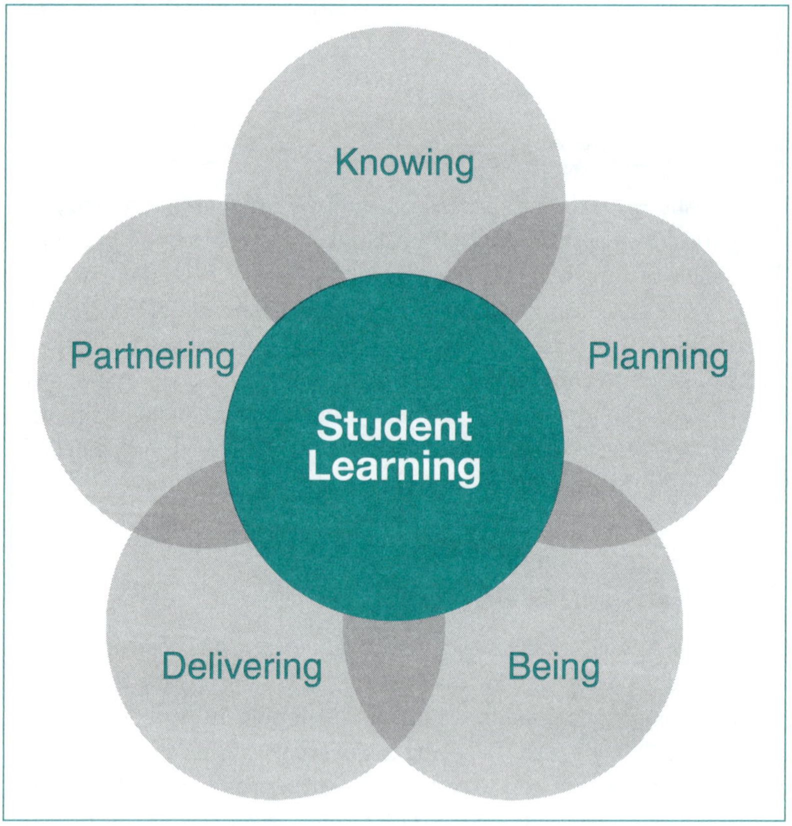

Source: Figure layout by Bill Grimmer.

Ms. Samson's integrated practice can be examined through five lenses: knowing, planning, being, delivering, and partnering, represented in Figure 7.1. Consider how each is present throughout her interactions with Danielle.

Knowing. Ms. Samson knows Danielle well enough to identify that she is distressed. She pays attention to clues that let her know how Danielle is doing. She also is careful not to interpret Danielle's actions as apathy. Ms. Samson is also familiar with the fact that Danielle has goals for her education, which, as her teacher, she wants to support in any way that she can. Ms. Samson knows that her belief in Danielle and her goals is critical to Danielle's success. Ms. Samson believes that the work she does on behalf of each student makes a difference in their educational outcomes, such as understanding the content, developing self-efficacy, persisting, and attending. She demonstrates *teacher efficacy*; in other words, a "sense of competence" that what she does as a teacher impacts Danielle's learning outcomes (Protheroe, 2008). As one of many students in the classroom, Danielle participates in a learning community that values personalization as a critical component of readiness to learn. Frequent formative assessments, in addition to summative assessments, provide information that paints the whole picture of who Danielle is as a person and scholar.

Ms. Samson's teacher toolkit includes skills derived from a knowledge base about trauma-informed practices. Five years ago, she read excerpts from *Helping Traumatized Children Learn* (Cole, Eisner, Gregory, & Ristuccia, 2005) as part of a whole-faculty professional learning activity. She and the other teachers have ongoing opportunities to explore and further define how their classrooms, and the school, both anticipate and respond to trauma and chronic stress faced by their dynamic student body. In moments like these with Danielle, Ms. Samson's prior knowledge and foundational practices from day one of the school year—such as rituals and routines, as well as clear expectations and boundaries—provide stability when circumstances create dysregulation.

Planning. Ms. Samson has a revision policy in place that anticipates the irregularities of situations like Danielle's, while providing accommodation for her to be successful through an alternative pathway. Because of this, Danielle will have further opportunities to demonstrate what she knows and is able to do. This practice affirms the belief that her persistent effort will provide results. In addition to policy, there is clear communication about course expectations regarding student participation in order not only to understand content, but also to operate effectively in the classroom—both aspects of the learning community are shared in the syllabus and on the class website. Any update is readily accessible, which allows Danielle to plan for making up work and seeking assistance.

Lastly, Ms. Samson plans for students to be active participants through the high-interest curriculum she selects, paired with the hands-on, student-centered activities she designs. She puts emphasis on providing learning opportunities in which students will want to participate, since student engagement is perennially a professional learning goal of hers. She consistently thinks about transferring responsibilities to the students by asking herself, *What am I doing that* students *could be doing instead?* The answer to this question often includes asking questions, conducting experiments, solving problems, capturing data, computing results, reading related articles, maintaining materials, and cleaning up the room.

Being. Danielle is in a dysregulated state due to her acute stress. Although Ms. Samson could vicariously experience Danielle's trauma, she is aware of her own response to student suffering; therefore, she is prepared to *be* calm, *be* consistent, and *be* kind. Although she is empathetic, she is deeply concerned—deeply saddened, even— yet she does not show it. She knows that, as the adult most responsible for preserving a classroom climate that is stable, she must *be* regulated herself. After school, she plans to go for a run, followed by spending time with her family and unplugging. She intentionally leaves her worry about Danielle, and other school-related issues, at school. It's a self-care practice that she has been focusing on for the past two years. Whenever her stress is particularly high, she journals before leaving school and will check in with a peer or school counselor. Her own well-being is a priority. She has learned through experience that it must be so if she is going to be both effective for Danielle and the other students and loving to herself.

Next, she offers to be present with Danielle through her struggle by meeting with her for tutoring and checking in. She stays in her role as Danielle's teacher. She operates within a boundary that directs her to not pry or try to solve Danielle's problems that live outside her sphere of influence or appropriateness. Additionally, she encourages Danielle to care for herself through self-care practices that are emphasized by the entire school community. Both students and adults have learned about self-care through classes, advisement, assemblies, and professional learning opportunities.

Finally, it is said that a student's learning conditions are the teacher's working conditions. There is a definite parallel process existing within school environments: If teachers are happy, so are students; if students are stressed during a certain time of year, teachers are stressed at the same time; if teachers are focused on the state test, students are too; if teachers are calm, students follow their lead.

Delivering. Danielle's comfort level in class is the result of her familiarity with the flow of the class period—there is a distinct beginning, middle, and ending. She recognizes the way time is consistently organized. Class begins on time and ends on time. As a significant factor that contributes to the tenor of a classroom culture, time is monitored by both the teacher and the students. Danielle is aware of how much time is allocated for the tasks as clearly outlined by Ms. Samson for tasks like answering warm-ups, group work, solving problems, and writing responses. Therefore, she can make decisions about how to spend her time. This lends itself to her locus of control over both the time and the task. If she needs more time, she asks for it. Ms. Samson is aware of time and how students are spending it, allowing her to monitor and adjust as dictated by the learning made evident in what students are doing.

Within the routines of the classroom, Danielle experiences a variety of learning formats—whole-group, small-group, and individual. She is able to demonstrate what she knows by making her learning visible through written, verbal, and performance tasks. She writes her response to the warm-up, writes her answers to the quiz, solves problems, converses with her team, reflects on her progress, explains her thinking, and asks questions. In doing so, she makes meaning for herself and demonstrates her knowledge and skill on any given day. She is doing the work of a learner; she is at the center of her learning.

Partnering. Ms. Samson knows that supporting Danielle through a crisis is not her role alone. She relies on other available resources, such as school-based counseling and connection with other teachers. Ms. Samson collaborates with a team of colleagues who approach student well-being with similar integrated practices at her school. She can rely on them to show Danielle similar care while helping Danielle persist in her responsibilities as a student. First, Ms. Samson checks in with both Mr. Anderson and Ms. Cummings at lunch that day. She is aware that they are also Danielle's teachers this semester, and she wants to connect about what she has observed today and share ideas about next steps. They too observed Danielle's distress, and the three of them share what they are doing to offer her assistance, such as tutoring and revisions. They agree that Ms. Samson will place a counseling referral for Danielle that day. Ms. Samson also considers touching base with Danielle's parents. Although she willingly contacts parents in various situations, she decides to wait a couple days and see. She will encourage Danielle to talk to her mom and dad about the stress she is under and connect with them about ideas they may have. Finally, she sends an email to Mr. Simms, the assistant principal, with whom she frequently collaborates in order to offer students support. He often helps keep an eye on students who are having pronounced struggles and may need additional help.

Several years ago, Ms. Samson's school did not have much building-based capacity for school counseling. The school had a district psychologist who traveled between four schools monitoring a big caseload of students. Other than the psychologist, the three guidance counselors were expected to manage acute student behavioral or mental issues, as was the assistant principal, if available. As the school grew in its awareness of effective practices in adolescent mental health and trauma-sensitivity, the demand for building-based counseling resources grew. This priority area motivated teachers and administrators to seek resources from community partners in the form of funding, expertise, and services. This allowed the school to hire mental health counselors with training and the capacity to support more students. It also provides students and families more intense support services through outside organizations. And, in Ms. Samson's case, the increased capacity offers her a place to garner resources in serving students while attending to her own need for support.

Foundation for the Integrated Learning Model #1: Social Capital

Personal and professional connections matter to personal well-being. *Whom* we know often overshadows *what* we know in terms of building connection. Social networks, both in and out of school, often provide the resources, know-how, and support needed to achieve a goal, whether it be losing those extra 10 pounds, scheduling a speaker, or finding a new job. Social connections and all that they offer matter more deeply, however, to a growing adolescent's sense of self and belonging. Teenagers' perception that they are accepted and valued comes from the people around them. Further, having a network—crew, gang, group, sisterhood—forms a foundation from which to build their dreams. In the absence of such foundations, people can experience isolation. Believing that you are alone in the world with no one to help you and no resources from which to garner support or opportunity predicates a loss of self-efficacy. What you do to let your students know that they are valued and that help is available matters.

Foundation for the Integrated Learning Model #2: Self-Efficacy

Beliefs drive our actions. What is a belief, really? Beliefs are thoughts or ideas that we deem to be true. This is interesting, because we go through our everyday lives believing our thoughts as truth, rarely challenging or being curious about them. For example, a student shows up late to class and the teacher believes she just doesn't care. Or someone in a fancy car cuts you off in traffic and you believe that wealthy people think they are entitled to break the rules. Beliefs are deeply rooted in the psyche as a way of organizing and making sense of one's environment, perceptions, and experience. They are shortcuts. Rather than fact-check a belief, the brain just fills in the gaps of missing information as a time-saving tool: If A happened, then B must be true (Lewis, 2018).

If habits are brain-energy savers, as mentioned in Chapter 3, then so too are beliefs. Beliefs are like habits of mind, in that they condense similar experiences and environmental stimuli to create shortcuts that conserve mental energy. As kids, we listen to and learn from parents or authority figures. What a time-saver, to not have to figure everything out by yourself every time. Beliefs help maintain the status quo, which saves energy; no threat, no change, homeostasis of system (Lewis, 2018). While creating your personal beliefs is easy, changing them is hard. Changing a belief requires the full engagement of the brain to essentially rework the entire system (physical, emotional, spiritual). It is much easier to ignore new information that challenges a belief than it is to reorganize your whole system. That is why people can stay stuck in a belief no matter what evidence, experience, or proof exists that challenges its validity. Often when we think we are reasoning, we are actually rationalizing our world to fit with our current beliefs (Mooney, 2011).

Naming these beliefs, in a classroom or as a school, can and should involve a process where everyone has a voice to wrestle with issues like equity, legacy, fairness, and capacity and, more important, where everyone has a shared vision. Identifying belief systems in your school requires asking tough questions like "Who are we?" (which isn't always in line with who we want to be). Or "What do we, as a community, believe?" and "Are our actions in line with our beliefs? If not, what needs to change?" Collective efficacy informs your school community, and each member within it, of what is possible for students and adults alike.

Foundation for the Integrated Learning Model #3: Locus of Control

Beliefs are also connected to a sense of control and whether you believe that control resides inside or outside of yourself. People who have an internal locus of control are those who believe that they are responsible for and have control over decisions, efforts, outcomes, and basically their own life. Educational practitioners refer to this as *agency*—essentially, one's ability to exercise voice, choice, and ownership in learning activities and outcomes as a result of possessing self-efficacy. Albert Bandura (1997) forged the connection between student agency and efficacy, offering the important concept that beliefs and actions about one's own ability can impact one's resulting life experiences. One must begin with belief and then be able to act.

To the contrary, an external locus of control dictates a belief system where a person's life is controlled by external factors such as fate, luck, and other outside forces. In education, these forces include parents, society, technology, social media, and politics—all things outside the school's control. Generally, people with an external locus of control experience increased anxiety, feelings of powerlessness, and lack of agency. This makes sense, because they often feel like they are at the mercy of external factors they cannot influence (Joelson, 2017). Imagine how this might manifest in a classroom for students who feel little sense of control. You probably know how it feels when *you* have little control over circumstances at school or at home. Here is one simple exercise to help you identify where you have agency to make change and where you don't: Draw a line down the middle of a sheet of paper. On one side of the line, make a list of things you have control of. On the other side, make a list of things you do not have control of.

Taking the Integrated Model School-Wide

Schools are places where people come together in pursuit of doing good work for good purposes. Education is a higher calling, because it points to a purpose greater than ourselves, whether that purpose be opportunity, freedom, democracy, or progress. Certainly not every student arrives at your buildings at the same place academically, physically, developmentally, or socially. Each student brings his or her strengths hand in hand with his or her weaknesses. Your students who have experienced chronic stress or trauma arrive at school with needs that require your community to understand them and, subsequently, to respond in effective ways. There are several areas to consider in leading an integrated student learning model such as the one put forth in this book.

Build Collective Efficacy

This integrated approach matters, and believing it—for yourself individually, and as a school community—will make a difference for students. Beliefs about students direct actions toward students. Therefore, exploring beliefs about students and student learning requires bravery, because sometimes doubt flows beneath the surface of speech and behavior. When addressing potential disbelief about what students are capable of—or your own disbelief about what you are capable of—it is easy to make excuses and place blame. You and other teachers may have thoughts, for example, that point at being unprepared for the entirety of the job ("I wasn't trained for this") or your mismatch of fit for the job ("If only I was at another school, it would be easier"). The problem in this type of thinking is that underlying beliefs about kids and a teacher's ability to productively and positively impact them have the potential to negatively impact them.

When schools as a whole fail to believe in student ability and possibility, it's nearly impossible to see positive student outcomes. In fact, since *collective* efficacy is shown to have the most significant impact (effect size), $d = 1.57$, on student achievement of all 252 factors studied by John Hattie and his team (2018), the opportunity to develop and sustain collective efficacy is simply not one that teachers and leaders can overlook.

Most important, your beliefs about students impact what they believe about themselves. If educators believe students can succeed, students will believe they can too. If you don't, they won't. It's a powerful proposition when you consider this dynamic in teaching and learning. In her seminal work *Collective Efficacy* (2017), Jenni Donohoo referred to this as the Pygmalion Effect (p. 17). If student efficacy, and ultimately student agency, is a goal of education, then digging into teacher beliefs is a worthy exploration. In fact, it is an investment in student outcomes. School-wide beliefs start with each member of the school community.

Educators, like most people, have a tendency to lose faith when it's difficult to see the results of effort and dedication. Like other professionals, we tend to *believe it when we see it*. It's for this reason that leadership should promote opportunities for teachers to observe students doing work that was not thought possible. For example, how might teachers observe students like Danielle working effectively in a small group and engaging at high levels? How might they have an opportunity to examine written student work in order to identify student ability and drive instructional practice? Or how might teachers get to hear students present their work to the community? The sooner teachers can connect effective teaching strategies with positive outcomes, as in Figure 7.2, the more likely they will be to use them again.

Figure 7.2   Methods of Building Collective Efficacy

- Students present their work products.
- Students showcase their assets—what they are good at.
- Students name what makes them successful.
- Teachers collaboratively examine student work.
- Teachers observe students at work in classrooms.
- Teachers identify and use high-leverage practices in teaching and learning.
- Leaders challenge their beliefs about student learning, teacher learning, and leading.
- Leaders model their beliefs.
- Leaders provide professional learning opportunities to investigate beliefs.
- Leaders use methods to build collective efficacy—*seeing is believing.*

Because daily informative assessment focuses on student growth within small units of instruction, it's possible for teachers (and students) to identify those instructional strategies that correlate to specific outcomes. Using this method of determining cause and effect, leaders can focus their efforts on high-leverage practices, such as conferring and small-group instruction, to increase student achievement.

Finally, the journey to building collective efficacy includes building partnerships. Collective impact is stymied when this important work of teaching and learning is conducted in isolation. Teachers and leaders need one another, respectively and collectively, in order to make an impact on student learning. Additionally, it's essential to partner with external organizations that can provide for students and families in ways that schools cannot—in the areas of health care, mental health services, financial resources, employment, internships, and so on.

Build a Mental Health Counseling Department

Ideally, schools should have fully staffed counseling departments to help students, staff, and administrators deal with the impact of trauma and chronic stress. In this integrated model, school counselors provide professional learning to staff in order to help integrate the mental wellness aspect of education. If your school doesn't have a budget for counselors, think creatively about how you can attend to the mental wellness of your school and share its priority. Partnering with local community mental health centers, creating referral lists for resources in the community, writing grants to fund positions, and working with local universities to arrange internships for students in their counseling programs are low-cost ways to connect with community resources while you work to fund and build a department.

Prioritize Integration

Leading is a relentlessly demanding job. As a school leader, you know that there are vying requests for your limited time, and there is only so much bandwidth you can offer a myriad of school-based and district-based initiatives. It is necessary to determine whether the integrated model outlined is this book is worth the reallocation of resources. The increasing focus on social and emotional learning across the United States indicates that education must consider the comprehensive needs of our students. Placing emphasis on the whole child in the context of high-leverage practices in teaching and learning fosters an integration of education and student formation that will lead to beneficial outcomes for students.

Something must go in order to prioritize a focus such as this. As other schools find value in this model, it becomes easier to say no to initiatives and programs that don't support an integrated model, like segregated efforts to incorporate social and emotional learning without addressing the core of a teacher's job—curriculum design, instructional delivery, and assessment use. Frankly, the more embedded effective mental health practices are within the regular course of teaching and learning practices, the fewer supplemental initiatives are needed. Ideally, general course offerings and mental health services are designed to serve each student in meaningful and holistic ways that mirror best practices in both psychosocial and educational fields.

Leadership is the linchpin to student success. You have a remarkable opportunity to make a lasting impact on the lives of students by offering hope and a place of possibility through this type of integrated education.

Reflections

As you put together the elements of an integrated teaching, learning, and mental health model, consider the following questions:

1. How do I describe an integrated model of student well-being with effective teacher practices?

2. In what specific areas do I see the most opportunity for growth as a teacher?

3. With whom can I forge partnerships, if I haven't done so already?

4. What do I really believe about my students, collectively and individually?

5. In what ways don't I believe I can make an impact?

(Continued)

(Continued)

6. How can my school better cultivate an integrated model of teaching, learning, and mental health for both students, and adults?

____

____

____

Toolkit for Tomorrow

As I integrate practices in teaching, learning, and mental health, I can:

❑ know my students well, as scholars and adolescent people.

❑ plan curriculum, instruction, and assessment that use effective practices in mitigating the effects of trauma and chronic stress.

❑ be calm, centered, and consistent.

❑ understand what I can control and what I cannot.

❑ deliver instruction that is student-centered.

❑ start a practice of noticing my beliefs and challenging them when necessary.

❑ partner with fellow teachers, counselors, administration, parents/families, and outside organizations to support myself and my students.

❑ act in kind and loving ways.

❑ integrate what I know about mental health and high-leverage teaching practices.

❑ lead with compassion . . . for myself and for others.

In the End, Be Loving

You can do this. Bringing together effective practices in teaching and learning with those in mental health will give you an opportunity to connect with students in such a way that cultivates learning at all levels. Believe that what you do *every day,* in both big and small ways, truly impacts your students' lives. It takes humility. It takes courage. Most importantly, it takes the love of educators to do the scope of work that serves the student as both a person and a scholar. As Stephen Covey stated so beautifully, if you "live the law of love," then the right decisions will be readily apparent (2004).

References

Almarode, J., & Vandas, K. (2018). *Clarity for learning: Five essential practices that empower students and teachers.* Thousand Oaks, CA: Corwin.

American Counseling Association. (2011). *Fact sheet #9: Vicarious trauma.* Retrieved from https://www.counseling.org/docs/trauma-disaster/fact-sheet-9---vicarious-trauma.pdf

Atwell, N. (2015). *In the middle: A lifetime of learning about writing, reading, and adolescents.* Portsmouth, NH: Heinemann.

Bandura, A. (1997). *Self-efficacy: The exercise of control.* New York, NY: Freeman.

Brown, B. (2012). *Daring greatly: How the courage to be vulnerable transforms the way we live, love, parent, and lead.* New York, NY: Gotham Books.

Brown, B. (2018). *Dare to lead: Brave work. Tough conversations. Whole hearts.* New York, NY: Random House.

Centers for Disease Control and Prevention. (2019). *About the CDC-Kaiser ACE study.* Retrieved October 5, 2019, from https://www.cdc.gov/violenceprevention/childabuseandneglect/acestudy/index.html

The Choices Program. (2019). *Debating U.S. drone policy.* Brown University. Retrieved October 12, 2019, from https://www.choices.edu/teaching-news-lesson/debating-u-s-drone-policy/

Cole, S. F., Eisner, A., Gregory, M., & Ristuccia, J. (2005). *Helping traumatized children learn (volume 1): Creating and advocating for trauma-sensitive schools.* Boston, MA: Massachusetts Advocates for Children.

Covey, S. (2004). *The 7 habits of highly effective people: Powerful lessons in personal change.* New York, NY: Free Press.

Diaz, C. I. (2018, August 20). The truth about teacher burnout: It's work induced depression. *Psych Learning Curve.* Retrieved from http://psychlearningcurve.org/the-truth-about-teacher-burnout

Donohoo, J. (2017). *Collective efficacy: How educators' beliefs impact student learning.* Thousand Oaks, CA: Corwin.

DuFour, R., & Eaker, R. (1998). *Professional learning communities at work: Best practices for enhancing student achievement.* Bloomington, IN: Solution Tree Press.

Duhigg, C. (2014). *The power of habit: Why we do what we do and how to change.* New York, NY: Random House Trade Paperbacks.

Dweck, C. S. (2008). *Mindset: The new psychology of success.* New York, NY: Ballantine Books.

Economic Policy Institute (EPI). (2018, April 29). Average teacher salary down 4.5 percent, NEA report finds [News release]. Retrieved from http://www.nea.org/home/74876.htm

Edmondson, A. C. (2019). *The fearless organization.* Hoboken, NJ: John Wiley & Sons.

Evans, K., & Vaandering, D. (2016). *The little book of restorative justice in education: Fostering responsibility, healing, and hope in schools.* New York, NY: Good Books.

Forbes, H. T. (2012). *Help for Billy: A Beyond Consequences approach to helping children in the classroom.* Boulder, CO: Beyond Consequences Institute.

Gallagher, K. (2006). *Teaching adolescent writers.* Portland, ME: Stenhouse Publishers.

Hammond, Z. (2015). *Culturally responsive teaching and the brain: Promoting authentic engagement and rigor among culturally and linguistically diverse students.* Thousand Oaks, CA: Corwin.

Hattie, J. (2012). *Visible learning for teachers & students: How to maximise school achievement.* London, England: Routledge.

Hattie, J. (2018). *Hattie's updated list of factors related to student achievement: 252 influences and effect size.* Retrieved from https://visible-learning.org/hattie-ranking-influences-effect-sizes-learning-achievement

Haynes, M. (2014). *On the path to equity: Improving effectiveness of beginning teachers.* Washington, DC: Alliance for Excellent Education.

Ingersoll, R., Merrill, L., & Stuckey, D. (Updated 2014). *Seven trends: The transformation of the teaching force.* Philadelphia, PA: CPRE. Retrieved from https://eric.ed.gov/?id=ED566879

Jensen, E. (2013). *Engaging students with poverty in mind: Practical strategies for raising achievement.* Alexandria, VA: ASCD.

Jensen, F. E., & Nutt, A. E. (2016). *The teenage brain: A neuroscientist's survival guide to raising adolescents and young adults.* New York, NY: Harper.

Joelson, R. B. (2017, August 2). Locus of control [Web log post]. *Psychology Today.* Retrieved September 11, 2019, from https://www.psychologytoday.com/us/blog/moments-matter/201708/locus-control

Katherine, A. (1991). *Boundaries: Where you end and I begin.* Park Ridge, IL: Parkside Publishing.

Lerner, H. G. (2017). *Why won't you apologize? Healing big betrayals and everyday hurts.* New York, NY: Simon & Schuster.

Lewis, R. (2018, October 7). What actually is a belief? And why is it so hard to change? [Web log post]. *Psychology Today.* Retrieved September 10, 2019, from https://www.psychologytoday.com/us/blog/finding-purpose/201810/what-actually-is-belief-and-why-is-it-so-hard-change

McGee, P. (2017, November 28). The low blow of labels. *Corwin Connect.* Retrieved October 5, 2019, from https://corwin-connect.com/2017/11/low-blow-labels

Minor, C. (2019). *We got this: Equity, access, and the quest to be who our students need us to be.* Portsmouth, NH: Heinemann.

Mooney, C. (2011, May/June). The science of why we don't believe science. *Mother Jones.* Retrieved October 2, 2019, from https://www.motherjones.com/politics/2011/04/denial-science-chris-mooney

Morrison, T. (1992). *Jazz.* New York, NY: Knopf.

Moss, C. M., & Brookhart, S. M. (2012). *Learning targets: Helping students aim for understanding in today's lesson.* Moorabbin, Victoria: Hawker Brownlow Education.

MyPBLWorks (Buck Institute for Education). (n.d.). *A civilized world.* Retrieved from https://my.pblworks.org/project/civilized-world

National Center for Education Statistics. (2014). *Fast facts: Back to school statistics (372).* Retrieved from https://nces.ed.gov/fastfacts/display.asp?id=372

Nixon, C. (2016). CORE: What adolescents (or teenagers) need to thrive | Charisse Nixon | TEDxPSUErie | Penn State Behrend [Video file]. Retrieved October 5, 2019, from https://behrend.psu.edu/video/28322/2017/07/03/core-what-adolescents-or-teenagers-need-thrive-charisse-nixon-tedxpsuerie

Patterson, K., Grenny, J., McMillan, R., & Switzler, A. (2012). *Crucial conversations: Tools for talking when stakes are high.* New York, NY: McGraw-Hill.

Protheroe, N. (2008, May/June). Teacher efficacy: What is it and why does it matter? *Principal,* 42–45.

Ren, D., Wesselmann, E. D., & Williams, K. D. (2018). Hurt people hurt people: Ostracism and aggression. *Current Opinion in Psychology, 19,* 34–38.

Richardson, J. (2017, November). Using controversy as a teaching tool: An interview with Diana Hess. Originally published in December 2017/January 2018, *Phi Delta Kappan, 99*(4), 15–20. Retrieved October 10, 2019, from www.kappanonline.org

Ruiz, M., & Mills, J. (2008). *The four agreements.* Thorndike, ME: Center Point.

Serravallo, J. (2019). *A teacher's guide to reading conferences.* Portsmouth, NH: Heinemann.

Siegel, D. J. (2010). *The mindful therapist: A clinician's guide to mindsight and neural integration.* New York: W. W. Norton & Company.

Siegel, D. J. (with Bryson, T. P.). (2011). *The whole-brain child: 12 revolutionary strategies to nurture your child's developing mind.* New York, NY: Delacorte Press.

Siegel, D. J. (2013). *Brainstorm: The power and purpose of the teenage brain.* New York, NY: Penguin Group.

Sizer, T. R. (2004). *Horace's compromise: The dilemma of the American high school.* New York, NY: Houghton Mifflin.

Sparks, S. D. (2017, June 7). How teachers' stress affects students: A research roundup. *Education Week Teacher.* Retrieved from https://www.edweek.org/tm/articles/2017/06/07/how-teachers-stress-affects-students-a-research.html

Sporleder, J., & Forbes, H. T. (2016). *The trauma-informed school: A step-by-step implementation guide for administrators and school personnel.* Boulder, CO: Beyond Consequences Institute.

Sweeney, D. (2019). *Stumbling blocks to effective listening practices.* Retrieved from Google Docs on October 1, 2019.

Toch, T. (1991). *In the name of excellence: The struggle to reform the nation's schools, why it's failing and what should be done.* Oxford, OH: Oxford University Free Press.

Tovani, C. (2011). *So what do they really know? Assessment that informs teaching and learning.* Portland, ME: Stenhouse Publishers.

Ueland, B. (1992). *The art of listening.* Retrieved from http://traubman.igc.org/listenof.htm

U.S. Department of Education. (2019). *Common core state standards initiative.* Retrieved from www.corestandards.org

Vygotsky, L. S. (1978). *Mind in society: The development of higher psychological processes.* Cambridge, MA: Harvard University Press.

Wiggins, G. P., & McTighe, J. (2008). *Understanding by design.* Alexandria, VA: ASCD.

Williams, D. (2018). *Embedded formative assessment: Strategies for classroom assessment.* Bloomington, IN: Solution Tree Press.

Zehr, H. (2002). *The little book of restorative justice.* Intercourse, PA: Good Books.